RESCUE YOUR
MOM

This book is meaningless
unless you are moved to action.

RESCUE YOUR

MOM

Pradeep Kumar Singha

ZORBA BOOKS

ZB

ZORBA BOOKS

Published in India by Zorba Books, 2017

Website: www.zorbabooks.com
Email: info@zorbabooks.com

Copyright © Pradeep Kumar Singha

ISBN Print Book - 978-93-86407-67-2
ISBN eBook - 978-93-86407-68-9

Zorba Books Pvt. Ltd.(opc)
Gurgaon, INDIA

Printed at Repro Knowledgecast Limited, Thane

Dedicated to

Mother Earth
(Mother of all Life)

and

all the humans, animals, and trees
who have lost their lives directly or indirectly because of us.

Acknowledgements

I would like to express my gratitude towards **all the people** who have either directly or indirectly helped me in writing and making of this book, which is now being read by everyone the world over. I would like to thank all my teachers, including my parents who have always been there for me through their teachings and effort to make me a better human being; without which, I never would have developed an understanding of what is good and what is bad in life. I would like to thank one of my oldest friends **Soumya Gupta** who has always been there to strengthen my confidence in writing and completing this book, as well as giving her precious time for making quick corrections to the book even on her busiest days, and my friend **Manoj Kumar Samad** who has always been there for proofreading and to give me valuable suggestions, even sacrificing his sleep after a full day at work. In fact, over the past few years, he as well as **Ranjan Kumar**, have been the ones to patiently listen to hours of monologues from me on how we are harming the environment and what can be done about it. This helped clear my thinking and gave me confidence to undertake this endeavour—to write a book that I hope will influence people to make the required changes to save our Mother Earth!

I would like to thank **Sir David Frederick Attenborough** who had lent his voice to the TV show *"Planet Earth"*. It has influenced me all my life concerning how I see nature. In fact, I have been grateful to the entire team of *Planet Earth* for revealing the incredible beauty of nature and all forms of life that exist on our planet. This helped me understand the precious creations of nature we have on our planet and how they are important to the survival of human race; however, I was very young and studying in school then. I would also like to show my gratitude to the *late **Michael Jackson*** who I believe was a very good human being other than being the King of Pop. It was his songs like *"Heal the World"*, *"Earth Song"*, *"Man in the Mirror"*, *"Black or White"*, *"They don't Care About Us"*, and *"We Are The World"*, which showed me the way to be a better and caring human being rather than being selfish, greedy, violent, or jealous in life. And that is what also impelled me to write this book—to help people understand the same. He has been an inspiration to me in that even when you are alone, still you can do something big for this world, and you can be the change.

I would like to thank the entire team of the documentary film *"Before the Flood"*, especially **Mr. Leonardo DiCaprio**, who visits places throughout the world to explore the noticeable impact of global warming and climate change and looks for solutions. This finally made writing this book even more important than it has ever been so that we can all together make positive changes happen to save our planet from destruction. I would also like to thank **Mr. Arnold Schwarzenegger**, *Late Mahatma Gandhi*, and *Late Bruce Lee* whose valuable quotations matched my thoughts, for which I have mentioned them throughout this book.

I am grateful to the entire team of **Zorba Books Pvt. Ltd.**, especially my Consultant and the Editor in helping me express and shape my thoughts in an appropriate and organized way, as a book, making the best changes and valuable corrections, and for giving me an opportunity to customize my book, patiently waiting for my improvements for the book, and finally publishing this book, without which, nobody would have been reading it by now.

Two quite valuable persons — **Jonathan Guzi** (a talented *Concept Artist*) from San Francisco, U.S.A., and *Vanessa Gonzales* (author of *The Light in the Sound*) from Portland, Oregon, U.S.A., deserve my best gratitude for helping me out at the final stage by creating the beautiful cover for the book exactly as I wanted, and editing all the extra contexts that I had to add to the book, as well as for all her aspiring guidance and friendly advice for many topics covered in the book. Without that, this book probably wouldn't look the way it does now.

Lastly, a big thanks to ***my family*** who have been very supportive, for understanding my retreat into reading and writing day in and day out. Even when they did not know what I was actually doing, especially my dad who is quite serious about my career and hates me sitting on a laptop all the time, doing things that he doesn't understand. However, he never dissuaded me and believed that I would do something good. And all this would never have been possible without ***my mom***—the one who made everyone in my family have faith in me and funded the publishing of this book. Yes, my mom helps me in saving our biggest mom—Mother Earth! Not only my mom, but my dad and my brother also contributed to it at the final stage by helping me with every assistance I needed right on time.

I am also grateful to the **Lightstairs® Entertainment Company** which is sponsoring this book, funding its marketing and global publicity, for providing pictures, supporting evidence, and illustrations for the book, for building its website, supporting the cause and the intention behind writing it. There is no doubt that I will always be thankful to one of the greatest research organizations in the world—*NASA (National Aeronautics Space Administration)*, one of my favourites, for bringing us the evidence of climate change and information about Global Warming mentioned throughout this book.

This book is the outcome of many people whom I have come across throughout my life, who influenced my life as well as gave me the power to influence others and the world. I could have never written this book had I not been listening to the messages that they had been and are still giving to people.

I would like to thank *you* the reader for both buying this book and reading it, and extending your valuable support to nonprofit organizations in order to save our Mother Earth from being exploited and deteriorated by the people of this world.

RECOGNIZE WHAT YOU KNOW NOT *and* DO WHAT YOU DO NOT

This should be a serious concern for all those who live on planet earth.

You look at this book as just another book dealing with the usual topics. Yes, indeed. It does contain a "usual topic", and that is what forms our biggest concern as we approach the end of our lives and this planet. You may not realize that what you may not see happening around you was already begun a decade ago at other places in this world. And you have been left to anticipate a holocaust that could have been prevented.

When anything happens to your mother, you are ready to do anything or go to any extent to restore her health. Right? Your Mother Earth has always been taking care of you and the entire human race, silently, without even being noticed. But did you ever spare a minute to at least pray for her? Your mom and dad would have never been able to raise you without the support of Mother Earth. She has always been there for all of us. But have you ever been there for her whenever she needed you the most? Today, she is facing the world's biggest challenges and problems that pose a dangerous threat to her existence, along with those humans, who, like responsible children, are fighting for her cause. These problems have not arisen of their own accord. Their occurrence stems from our greed and negligence. Now, our mother needs our help in putting everything back to how it was; to remedy all the damage that we have done to this planet. Being a responsible child, shouldn't you be engaging in the process? Isn't it your duty too? Your helpless "mom" awaits your response…

Before You Read

Even if you don't like reading books, I recommend that you read this one for the urgent message it shares with its readers. This is not the usual fiction or a book on environmental studies; this is a book on humanity and mankind, gathering support by engaging important and caring people like you. Be a part of a movement that we can all be proud of tomorrow. Start by giving this book a go.

Together we can make the change possible. Unless you rise, the rest will sleep on until calamity knocks at their door in the form of the deadliest forces ever faced before by mankind.

You are a person, I know, of whom we can all, one day, be really proud of and say with tears of gratitude, that you made a better day for this planet and its inhabitants. Now, if you are wondering—*"Man, I haven't even started doing anything yet of which the world can be proud of"*. Well then, your contribution has already begun right with the purchase of this book! And the "one day" is *today*—right now, as soon as you have started reading this book. With this single act, you show that you care to know what is happening around the world; what is causing its degradation, what the impact is and what steps to take to resolve the situation.

Don't worry, if you haven't paid for this book; even if you've borrowed it, found it on a shelf or in a dustbin, stolen it or downloaded a pirated version. All I want is to heighten your awareness, and once I have done that, a better tomorrow isn't far away.

The better tomorrow does not come for free,
it is an outcome of what we do today.

Contents

A Brief Introduction

Have you heard the term 'endangered species'? Yes. Then it's time you heard about an endangered planet: Earth.

Are you afraid of death? Do you realize how many people, animals, and trees we kill every day? Yes, you and I, all of us, are responsible for someone or something's death everyday and we are not even aware of it. That's because we are safe and we don't take any action until we see a devastating flood, tornado, hurricane, or a volcano, threatening complete destruction of everything that matters to us, including our life, which is our most precious possession. In fact, once we lose our possessions, we begin cursing the planet, cursing nature, cursing God, but how many times do we curse ourselves for such calamities? Nature has its own way of revealing the truth to us; it has always given us indications, made us aware that something isn't right, something isn't working, something is going wrong, but do we ever have any time or spare even a minute to examine which of our activities is causing a drastic change in the climate which is obviously going to impact our lives sooner, rather than later. Previously, I believed our actions were slowly degrading this planet and indeed, however, over the last decade, this has accelerated. We have made unbelievable progress in destroying the very firmament on which we live. It's time for a change.

Everything is possible only if we step forward to take action,
instead of simply doing nothing and claiming
that it's impossible.

Before I wrote this book, I wanted to donate funds to as many organizations throughout the world as possible. But then I thought, okay, so how many people are doing that already? I've decided to help the organizations in every way I can, because I am aware. I have also decided to improve the way I am, the way I work, the way I eat, the way I sleep, and the way I handle things, so that none of my activities are harmful to our planet or any of its beings—and all this is possible because of this awareness. But what about the rest of the people in this world? Many of them don't even know why these organizations exist, what problems we are facing, and what exactly we should be doing, because they are too busy with their own lives. And many who do have an inkling, still don't bother to act, because they don't notice anything wrong happening around them by which their lives are affected. By the time they become aware, it will be too late to take any action. By then, lives will be lost, cities will be devastated, and several species will have become extinct. Material wealth can be regenerated over time, but lives, once lost, can never be brought back again. Hence, *the time to act is now and not in the future. Act before your efforts become worthless.* Any delay in taking action will mean a loss to our planet that can never be compensated. *The sooner we act, the more we save, and increase the possibility of living on a healthy planet that will continue to sustain life.*

"If you spend too much time thinking about a thing,
you'll never get it done."

– Bruce Lee

I may not be a professional author, but what matters most is whether I can be a good and responsible human being. A human being is neither selfish nor careless. A mindful human always thinks about others first, and then about himself. And he finds pleasure in others' well-being, be they humans, animals or Planet Earth. It is a question you must ask yourself too. *Your actions define the kind of person you are.* So, keep observing and you will know what you really are. Only time will tell what we can really be in our life, a mindful human, or someone who inflicts pain upon others.

"To know oneself is to study oneself in action with another
person."

– Bruce Lee

What is the Issue?

We all know the climate on earth has been changing for quite a long time. You may have observed that on your TV or read about it in books and newspapers. But, since then, how much of that has actually penetrated your consciousness? How many of your daily activities have you cared to change, or what actions have you taken to stop perpetuating climate change? The fact is that most of us simply watch and read about climate change and forget everything the very next day. This is because *until we see something devastating happening in our own lives, we don't bother to act*. We believe we are quite safe in our homes—that whatever is happening is taking place in some other city or country, so there is nothing for us to be concerned about. But we are so wrong. The events occurring elsewhere are just an indicator—just the beginning, and sooner or later the catastrophe will be at our doorstep. By then, it will be too late. What is gone will be gone forever. Not lost in an act of God but through our own willful destruction and indifference.

All the calamities that happen around this world are mostly the results or byproducts of our own interaction with nature. Therefore, if you want to stop it, start by improving your activities.

If you still don't really know what global warming or climate change is all about, you may kindly refer to the chapter "**Global Warming and Climate Change**" in this book.

In short, **global warming** is the increase of the Earth's average surface temperature due to the effect of greenhouse gases, such as carbon dioxide emissions from burning fossil fuels or from deforestation, which trap the heat that would otherwise escape from Earth. This has been causing the global climate to change with noticeable consequences evidenced by the rise in sea level, global rise in temperatures, warming oceans, shrinking ice sheets, declining Arctic sea ice, glacial retreat, ocean acidification, decreased snow cover, the bleaching of coral reefs, stronger hurricanes and storms, extreme weather like very hot summers, chilling winters, floods, etc.

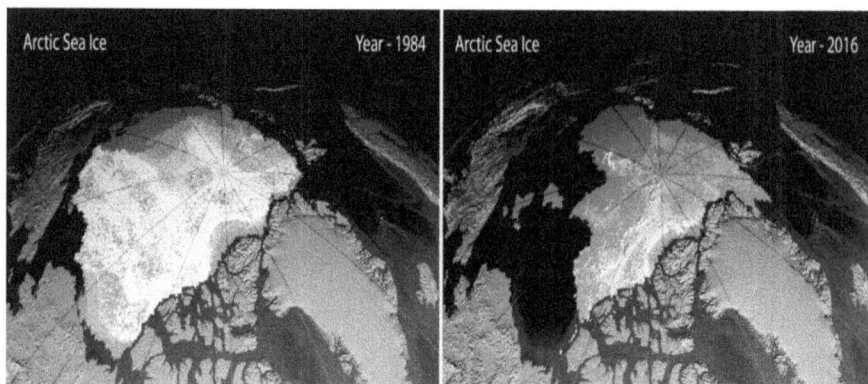

Older, thicker Arctic sea ice declines
September 1984 - September 2016
The area covered by Arctic sea ice at least four years old has decreased from
718,000 square miles (1,860,000 square kilometers) in September 1984 to 42,000
square miles (110,000 square kilometers) in September 2016.
Source: NASA Earth Observatory.
http://climate.nasa.gov/images-of-change

The **ice sheets** at polar ice caps have not just started melting, but have already disappeared to a great extent over the past decade. Every five years, hundreds of cubic kilometers of ice in Greenland melts into the oceans. This has exposed the dark inner surfaces of the glaciers, which in turn are now absorbing heat rather than reflecting it as they used to when they were covered completely in white snow. In this way, the rate of glacier melt is continuously increasing over time.

This has caused a considerable rise in **sea levels** which we usually ignore as we don't see it with our own eyes. The impact of this is evident in many coastal areas of the world where water has entered the cities and villages, and the homes of people there have been ruined. Small islands, especially, are suffering the most. They have hardly contributed anything to the rise in temperature and global warming, but yet they face suffering because of our activities. Global warming has also caused change in weather patterns all over the world with noticeable consequences like more devastating hurricanes, tornadoes, droughts, and severely hot summers, floods during rainy seasons, and unbearable cold weather during winters.

How are we still not aware of what is happening all around us? All of which has been brought to our attention by scientists, geologists, environmentalists, and conservationists who are working hard on this and trying to save this planet from forthcoming dangers. Even among the regular citizenry, there are those who are really concerned about these environmental changes and have united to right the wrongs we have done. But for real change, we need a majority of the people of this world to gain awareness and start making changes. This is no longer just a 'serious concern'. This should now become a **mission** for all of us, where every one of us has an equal worth and responsibility to achieve this desperately important goal. Whether you are a child, an adult, or a senior citizen witnessing this change, we can all contribute to saving our planet—our only majestic and magnificent home, where we have been raised, raised our children, and are waiting to see future generations do the same.

Imagine the day when all the **natural resources** on earth are used up. It will be quite fascinating to see how those businesses go on, the ones that thrive on exploiting these resources. Those people who have grown rich by doing this will learn that no matter how much money they spend, it will be too late to save themselves from the deadliest forces of nature. Nature doesn't rely on our money. It relies on our care, our attention, and our love. The planet works for all—whether one cares for it, like our forefathers did, or us, who seem hell-bent on its destruction.

We need to open our eyes, no matter what political leaders say or what business tycoons would have us believe. Believe in yourself. Do what is right for this planet. And don't be swayed by those who promise to make your life better at the cost of this planet, whose ultimate goal is enriching themselves at all costs.

The **petroleum** oil (crude oil) continues to be extracted from the earth's crust until all the reservoirs for oil dry up. It will take millions of years to recover what we have been exploiting for decades. Do you think we are using petroleum because we have no other alternatives? No way! We are using it because we prefer to rely on what is cheap, easy to get, easy on our pocket and easy to exploit. In reality, using this crude oil is more of a luxury today than a need, but by doing so, we are simply digging a grave for our future. We need to depend on something more reliable, something which is safe for us and our planet, and which promises a better future – **renewable and clean sources of energy**.

These are completely harmless, and they are never wasted when we use them, simply because we use only the energy stored within them and not the whole of their form. For instance, we use the force of the wind and not use up the wind itself. That's why they are called "renewable" sources. And they don't produce any harmful byproducts when used. There are alternatives available but we are neither trying them out nor putting them into use permanently in our lives. We have become so indifferent that we don't even bother to look at the solutions we have right in our hands. This is because it seems we do not want to make even the smallest effort to save our future and our planet that requires spending a little more time or dealing with even a minimal inconvenience.

We aren't polluting Nature, we are polluting our own
Home. We will have to suffer one day.

The same thing is happening with **coal**. Millions of tons of coal are being used daily in thermal power plants to generate electricity for us, and in various industries, to manufacture a variety of products that we use. Coal is limited. The supply will end one day, and then we will have to wait for another million years to get it back. In fact, everything on this planet is going to be used up if we do not stop consuming our resources the way we are right now. Even if we decrease the amounts being used, there won't be any significant change; consumption figures will still be huge. The only way is to completely stop this rampant consumption and reserve current stock for future emergency. The problem is not just limited to the cessation of supply but extends even further to the impact of using it in our daily lives. The burning of coal releases a massive amount of carbon dioxide in the atmosphere, which is the major cause of greenhouse effect and global warming. Thermal power plants use coal on a large scale to generate electricity for us. It is also used by manufacturing industries (that melt metal, glass, etc. using coal) to produce goods (various products) for us. Now, we think we don't know how to stop using these goods as we need them every day in our lives. Well, *there is a solution everywhere but only when we look for it*.

Coral organisms called polyps that live in tropical waters throughout the world, deep down in the oceans, are degrading rapidly. The whole environment there is turning into a thing of nightmares. It looks like a place where a volcanic eruption has occurred and everything has burned into structures of ashes—this is actually called coral bleaching which occurs when the marine algae that live inside corals die. The reason for their death is high levels of carbon dioxide in the atmosphere and in the water. In fact, they absorb a large amount of carbon dioxide from the atmosphere but now the levels have gone so high that they are not able to process this change anymore. Changes in temperature and pollution also causes corals to evict their boarders, leading to coral bleaching that can kill the colony if the stress is not mitigated.

Still, we have time. Look around—not just around your home, but at the whole planet. Rouse your mind and be aware. This will save your life as well as keep all others safe too. Always be aware of the changes that happen to this planet due to your activity. This will keep you alerted to the coming danger so that you can prevent it from happening, rather than wait for it to happen, and then consider looking for a solution.

We are all blindly running after **wealth,** aren't we? But I ask you, what the use of that enormous wealth is, when there is no life ahead. The wealth we are running after is nothing when compared to the wealth that we already have naturally on this planet. Conserve it instead of exploiting it. This wealth has a limit after which it will end and that will mean the end of our species and all life forms on earth. What is the benefit of making *money* at the cost of the earth's biodiversity? Once it's extinct, can it be brought back ever again? We are the creators of money; we can always create as much of it as we want, but the biodiversity of earth, once lost, cannot be recreated once again. It is lost forever.

> *"Earth provides enough to satisfy every man's needs,*
> *but not every man's greed."*
>
> *– Mahatma Gandhi*

Money or Earth's Biodiversity: On What Does Life Thrive?

When I was in school, I was always curious about doing new things. Such as, I had an idea that the steam from chimneys of power plants and factories can be reused to generate electricity. Any steam released as it is in the atmosphere is simply a loss or waste of energy (heat energy of about 540kcal that water acquires from burning coal or any other fuel to form steam) as it contains a lot of heat energy within itself that it releases into the atmosphere when it condenses back to water. But in those days, there was nobody acceptable to whom I could share my ideas on more efficient power plants. Hardly anybody was interested in innovation. And I had no contact with those who really were. Also, people felt that I was just a school child, so I shouldn't try to do something better than those who are already engineers. Obviously, that became a matter of ego. However, I still tried contacting many people and organizations working on energy, but I never received a reply. Yeah, if the idea had been about receiving tons of money in their account, then I guess a lot of people would have come forward to know how they could make more and more money at the click of a button. Obviously, when people were not interested in implementing new ideas into their systems or workflow, what could be done?

I was badly discouraged. What can you do for a world that is only concerned about earning money and nothing else? When whatever you do will be worth nothing to them unless you do something that helps them to earn more money than what they could ever have. ***Money is an invention that gave rise to many more problems than it actually solved.*** Today, our planet is in danger only because of its people who have always neglected or disregarded things that were much more important than running after money. No amount of money will be able to save us when we are attacked by a devastating Tsunami or a terrifying volcanic eruption. We should be running after something that really saves our lives, and not after what puts our lives more at risk and creates unwanted or unexpected problems.

When we open the door and step out of our home, what do we see? People moving in various directions with purposes in mind and motives to fulfill, but most of them are moving and struggling for one and only thing—money—what they call "earning livelihood". What have we made of our life? What have we turned this world into? Observe it. What and how *should* it have been? Think of it—where we should actually be heading, compared to where we have been. What has caused our own difficulties and struggles? Whom do we curse when we are the creators of our own problems? Are we fond of filling our lives with difficulties? If no, then why does our life sometimes seem to feel more like suffering than a worthwhile gift? Can't we figure out and stop what unworthy things have been happening here so that we can add more meaning to our life, and a meaningful purpose for it to be devoted to? Has our understanding of what's truly meaningful completely abandoned us?

When I open my door, I don't like looking at the inconsiderate and ignorant members of the human race—those who don't care about their own future on this planet, let alone the welfare of their children and grandchildren. I'd rather look at the trees, the clouds in the sky, the sun, and then breathe in fresh air that fills me with hope so that I start my day with new strength, inspiration, and confidence acquired from Mother Nature, to fulfill my motives and goals in life. I don't need to depend on money to live on this planet. Actually, no life on this planet *needs* money to survive or even thrive. Nature provides everything at no cost. The fact is that *if we take care of Nature, it will take care of us*. A question we should all ask ourselves is if we are here only to live? I don't live for earning name and fame; it's worth nothing in the grand scheme of things. No black hole in the universe would spare my life if I say that I am the owner of a great company or an honourable president of the most powerful country on a human world, or I have trillions of dollars in my bank account somewhere on planet earth. To nature, these mean nothing, and so to me it means nothing. I am and will always be a speck of dust in this universe, no matter what I posses with the passage of time. Why do we spend our lives acquiring possessions just to make each other jealous? Does anyone take their possessions to the grave? So are we not all equal no matter what physical possessions we amass while alive? Hence, being a human being is more fulfilling than anything else. This is the true form that Nature has given us, whose value has mostly been underestimated by us, and Nature has always liked to see us in that form. My life is not even an enjoyment! How do I enjoy when others are still in pain and suffering? Not just humans, but every other species is suffering because of humans.

The best thing that we can be in life is—a human being,
the most precious thing that we can possess is—life,
and the best job to do in this world is—serve others.

If I live, that is only for doing something that I have always wanted to do, that counts in history and in someone's life. Serve nature and nature will serve you. It is actually when you serve nature, you serve yourself. This is much better than the world that we have built upon money where every day of our life starts with and ends in money until death. If this is the life we are going to give to our children—to struggle just to exist, then consider that they shouldn't be coming to this planet, increasing unnecessary burden on its available resources. Every other species on this planet is doing the same thing—struggling to survive, and a million more doing the same is not going to make any difference, except in becoming a burden to this planet, and a threat to the lives of those who are already in the struggle.

When Prime Minister Narendra Modi started the process of demonetization in India, he did so for a very good purpose. God knows how many people died with shock and heart attacks; how many died standing on the queue, and how many died even after reaching the banks. I wonder what money actually meant to them. I know, for them, it was their whole life of hard work, but I believe their hard work was actually more valuable than the money they had received in exchange for their back-breaking hard work. We clearly saw what happens when we give so much value to money and just run after it day and night without caring for anything else, considering money to be everything that we can ever have and all that is necessary to live. I think today it is much easier to kill people than it has ever been; just destroy the money and people will be dead on their own! What a great magic! How did our lives become so dependent on this naturally valueless man-made thing? That to earn it, we spend our entire life, and when we lose it, we lose even our remaining life!

Money has no value on its own. It is our 'needs'—be they basic or luxurious that give money an unnecessary value—the source of everything. Money is in fact, not even the source of everything, as it doesn't produce anything of its own. We get what we want only in exchange for money and that too only from humans, and not from nature or any other species of this planet. Of course, we cannot live by eating money and drinking its awful juice; we cannot use it to cover our bodies as we do with clothes, and cannot even build our houses using just those pieces of premium paper and coins. But money helps us acquire those things that actually serve our purposes. By the way, to whom do we pay the money to, to get those beautiful things? To other people. And from where do other people get all these beautiful things? Obviously, from nature. And what nature is giving us humans is what it has been giving to every other organism on this planet free of cost. Then how can money become more important and valuable than nature and our lives? It is just meant to serve the purpose of exchange. Money itself is just paper and metal, and the sources of those are the trees and the planet's womb.

When you are sick, indeed money will help you purchase medicines, but it will be the good people and not money, who will take care of you. Yes, money can also be used to hire people to look after you; however, sometimes, it may happen where you hire people by flashing your cheque book, indirectly letting them know how rich you are, which in turn, may ignite a new love for money in those people's mind. This may give rise to a situation where, if you do not agree to their demands, they may soon turn into your one-stop solution for death! Then you feel worse when you come to understand that your life continues till you're able to fulfill their greed, and your life ends the day you lose your ability to fulfill any more demands. Thus, money that should be used to purchase medicines for you can also be used to purchase poison, causing you to be dead in seconds. But living beings who love you will never put poison in your mouth in place of medicines. Understand the difference; understand in what the actual value lies.

Money stands for nothing. It only stands for whatever it is being used for, good or not. Don't make money an essential part of your life or value it more than any life on earth. Limit it to being only a means of exchange and nothing more. Of course, money can make your life better, but it also has the power to make your life worse. In one way or the other, money has been the root cause for most of the problems faced by the human race, and is now beginning to threaten the lives of other living species that don't even understand the term "money".

However, on the other hand, money has solved many problems too. But is that money doing it all on its own—the good and the bad? Certainly, it's the people who are doing everything while money is simply driving them to where they are turning their wheels of life. ***Money forms the driving force, the thrust that propels you ahead but it is you who decides where to go.*** It is you who decides whether to use money for doing good or bad. So, money alone cannot be held responsible for any problems. It neither created nor solved any of them. What is being done is from our side, so we are the ones to be blamed. We just invented it without knowing how to use it wisely.

Eradicating money completely is possible. How? It will happen when this **world turns into a family**. A father will never ask his children to pay him for bringing them food to eat, neither will their mother who prepares it every day for them with so much of love and effort. Think of farmers who grow grains and vegetables for their children to eat who are actually agricultural scientists, doing research to find better fertilizers that help grow healthier crops. The relationship does not necessarily need to be that of a father and son, but can also be that of friends or other relatives. All we need is to **create the world's largest family ever, with strong bonding amongst people.**

This will also help us focus on our actual goals rather than concentrate on earning money. People will always choose to do what they love to do. There will be no compulsion to choose something that pays a higher wage but doesn't suit their interests. People will be free to choose jobs based on what they are passionate about. And obviously, **when we do what we like doing the most, we usually give our best.**

What do we need money for? Has a tree ever asked you to pay it a dollar before it drops a fruit into your hands? Has a cow, goat, or buffalo ever asked you to pay some beautiful currency notes before they gave you their milk? Has Mother Earth ever charged you a penny for fresh water? Never. I don't understand then, why humans have monetized everything on earth. Does everything belong only to them that they can turn nature's bounty into a business? I know, the answer will be that *the labour put in to make certain natural things usable and consumable* is what humans sell in the market in exchange for money. I know that clothes are not available readymade on trees. They have to be created by humans using raw materials from nature. So, in that way, they are doing work on it for which they charge a fee. Well, I know the economics, but why does that have to be a business and why not as responsibility; why not produce things with love and care as one would for their family? Father ploughs the field, his son sprinkles the seeds while the daughter waters them, and at last, they all eat the food happily when the mother cooks it with love. The same thing can happen among friends and a larger community. Everybody has a role in a family just like in a business. Then why do we make a business out of everything that sometimes breaks relationships and kills people?

"Real living is living for others."

– Bruce Lee

Today, the value of money has been elevated to such an extent that people don't even hesitate taking somebody's life to acquire it. Nobody knows who would cause your death to possess the money you own. I am not against money; I am against the narrow mindset of people when it comes to money. I would like to remind you again that **money is not "everything"** as you have been considering your whole life. It is indeed the source to get that *"everything"*, but when that *"everything"* will be destroyed just in the desire to earn money, then the value of money will turn right into zero, after which you will realize that all your life you did not recognize the actual value of the natural things and blindly ran after a man-made thing. **Money is so useless that it cannot take the place of even a single object in this whole universe.** Think again the next time when you start valuing money over everything else. Does it really deserve that importance? In every case, money should be either your second choice or your last one, because other beings and natural elements on this planet have more value and importance than money itself.

Money has value only as long as things remain that it can purchase, after which it becomes valueless.

It is for money that most people commit crimes, harm the environment, kill animals, and become a threat to their own lives. It may be the source of acquiring everything that humans sell but by itself it can never be that everything. So the people must recognize the value of *everything* and put it always above the value of money. Let money be what it actually is. The more we start giving it a value, the more we start threatening our own lives, and sometimes, everyone else's too.

> *"Money doesn't make you happy. I now have $50 million but I was just as happy when I had $48 million."*
>
> *– Arnold Schwarzenegger*

Actually, we all have equal rights to use things available on earth, but **we were never the owner of anything that was already available on this planet.** This planet belongs to all life forms that are living on earth and we alone can't be the ones to utilize it, making a business out of anything that comes in our hand or under our feet. This is the greatest ever mistake that man has made, and we are having to pay it back at the cost of our lives. I am so ashamed that despite being the most intelligent species on earth, we do not acknowledge that this planet was never meant just for our own use. It was never our property. It was and will always be our mother. *A mother can neither be sold nor purchased* and if you are exploiting your own mother then that's the most shameful act you can do.

Not only this, even life is being sold on our planet. People purchase people, which is a crime, as well as animals, which is a crime again, but people consider this legitimate, since they are themselves not the victim. Hence, the animals are sold on the open market while humans, more discreetly, through the human-trafficking method. The one who purchases these humans and animals become their owner! How could we sell something whose value can never be measured? The *life of any organism is not an object that can be measured, weighed, sold or purchased.* It seems we can just turn anything into a business be it life, reputation, education, earth—just anything that one can sell for money to others who want to acquire it at any cost. Together, we can stop this contamination from spreading. We must finish it before it finishes us. We need to purify our brain, heart, and soul to become what we ought to be as true human beings.

> *Loss of money is nothing when compared to loss of life, which is actually a loss of everything.*

Suppose I discovered the Pacific Ocean, would that make me the owner of that ocean? I just found it; I didn't create it. *Discovering something is an achievement, but that doesn't give us a license to declare it as our property.* Because if this was so, then the real owners of Pacific Ocean should have been the sharks, whales, and all the other varieties of fish and marine organisms that have been living there long before we appeared on this planet. And, for sure, they are not selling it to humans for money that they cannot even eat, which to them is neither tasty nor digestible.

Have you ever heard of a bird needing money to build its nest or to feed its chicks? Ever wondered how the other organisms on this planet are making their living even when they have no barter system or money? *There is still a lot for us to learn from nature.* This environment has everything that we need to make a living. But we give money more importance than the environment itself. Are we really making the best use of money? If we say money has been introduced to maintain a balance in the economy, then is it really the 'balance' that we have been maintaining by making rich people richer and the poor more impoverished? The economy seems more ruined by money than the ways that it has been beneficial to humans. If we didn't know how to use it to benefit everyone then we shouldn't have made it. ***Our invention is killing people because we never learned how to use it wisely.***

Every man should have a certain amount of money to make his living on this planet. It makes no sense that only the rich have the right to live well, and the rest die in poverty, hunger, and pain. Every one of us has an equal right on this planet, hence ***everyone should have access to an amount of money with which we can fulfill at least our basic needs, irrespective of whether we work for anyone or not***. It is our right. We cannot take this right away from anyone who is born on earth. We have no right to make it compulsory for anybody to work for us just so that he can earn money, yet barely survive, then die of poverty and starvation if he is not able to work. Once his basic needs are met, then he will be able to think of getting work that suits his needs, fulfills his passion, or adds to human progress. It is the extra money he earns as a result of his work which decides whether he will lead an average life or a luxurious one. There should be no poor people in this world. ***It is the shortage of money to meet basic needs that forces people to abandon their dreams and give money so much unnecessary importance that they want to earn it at any cost.*** This is what makes many people turn to crime. We know this quite well, but are we stopping it? It is the responsibility of all the governments to make money globally accessible and available to all the people of this world to help meet their basic needs at least. But are they really doing that?

> *"Government's first duty and highest obligation is public safety."*
>
> *– Arnold Schwarzenegger*

The system governing the flow of money is also not always helpful or beneficial. One man produces money by simply printing paper and putting on it the values he wants those pieces of papers to have. Then he makes other men work and pays them the lowest possible sum of money as salary. After which, he makes a demand for tax that will be debited from their already low salary and he says he needs this to build roads and hospitals for them in turn. We create the money, we make it necessary for others to earn. Then we tell them to return a specific part of it to us so that we can build something good and useful for them in turn. In this way, we are like beggars begging for our own money. This raises many questions about intelligence: whether we actually know how to lead a better life on earth. Are we making our life better or simply worse? Is education proving to be really useful to us? *"A dog running after its own tail"*—that is what we have been doing here. First, we create the money, and then we spend our entire life running after it. We are chasing financial freedom when really, we could produce everything we need to live with abundance with little financial investment. The problem is that we set ourselves up to have to buy what we need from everyone else when we could produce most of it ourselves. Yet we've lost the knowledge on how to produce those things for ourselves. Still, rich and poor people alike exist in this so-called "developed" world. And we call this our great economic system. We don't even realize how many people have died unnecessarily in this way because of our unreliable economic system.

The government is the creator of all money, yet it asks for money from the common people to solve problems, to do something better for this planet and save people's lives. It looks as if we have been playing a game here that should have been played only by kids. However, we are adults, but look at our system... We know quite well that we need to save our planet, its biodiversity, and the lives of the people, yet the government will look for funds from the common people to do so. But the government cannot generate enough money on its own to save people's lives and this planet in time. And this is not only in the case of the government. Just consider, we have to save a forest area from being cleared, or go on a rescue mission to save people or an animal, and we are told that we won't be paid for this, think how many of us would really go to save the forest or on the rescue mission. There is also another great example of this: A doctor will not undertake any treatment of a person who has had an accident, unless all the formalities and police enquires have been completed, and all his fees have been paid. He acts more like a business man than a doctor who doesn't undertake a project unless he is assured that he is going to benefit from that project and it is completely risk-free. The fees, agreements, and formalities become more important than saving the life of a person then. This is the "great" system that we have created. How helpful, isn't it!?

"The more we value things, the less we value ourselves."

– Bruce Lee

This shows how much we care for money as well as our procedures, even when it comes to saving the lives of people or this planet's biodiversity. What is the use of money if it becomes the cause of all deaths and cannot be used to save lives of the people when needed? Why can't we come out of our system when we know it is what hinders us in every step of doing what is right for this planet or saving the lives of its inhabitants? We haven't created a great system of working but a hindrance that will mostly hinder us from doing right things at the right time. We have been slow in saving our planet because of this system. If we were free to do anything to save this planet, including having access to all the resources on time, then you might not be reading this book, or watching the organizations struggling hard every day to make everything right on this planet. We are responsible for every creature that has ever died on this planet because of our system be it people, animals, or any form of life. Can money ever compensate for the loss of lives? Is it only money that is of concern to us? Has life and humanity no value? Aren't we more concerned about our systems and protocols at first than saving people, animals, and this planet? Haven't we made money unnecessarily compulsory at every step of human progress, be it saving lives, or doing something good for this planet's future? I have my answers, you need to find yours.

We are simply looping in a cycle; we cannot progress until we pull ourselves out of that cycle and consider something beyond that which lets us progress straightway in a specific direction instead of looping and progressing ahead. Most of our time and talent is wasted in simply continuing the cycle which adds hardly anything to the progress of humanity.

What has been said above can also be applied to our system of circulation of money. If all the governments—instead of waiting for taxes from the people—produced money on their own and put the funds directly into saving our planet, then I do not think anybody would have any problem with money being allocated for the welfare of our planet, including us. The governments just need to keep a record of how much funds have been spent on which project and when. They will never have to compromise with our planet's welfare because of insufficient funds accumulated through collection of taxes. Now that doesn't mean they will start filling up their ever-empty pockets when they can produce as much money as is required. All that is done should be for this planet and its inhabitants and not for any self-profit. This will also enable every nonprofit organization of the world to enforce every action they want to take on time to save this planet and we will never be late again. The government should be for the people and not for any business tycoons who pay in backroom bribes so that they can carry on with all their harmful activities on our planet at the cost of our lives and further deteriorate the environment for the future generations.

Collecting tax is good, but insufficient tax or a lack of funds cannot be an excuse for the loss of lives and biodiversity of this planet or for a country lagging behind in development. In such a case, people cannot be held responsible for what the government itself and its worthless system chooses to do. Sometimes getting out of the system to do something good isn't wrong when it is done for the welfare of the people and this planet.

I knew the value of everything right from the beginning of my life, and this is quite true. When I was just 3 years old, I still remember, the first time I valued money—it was for the hard work that the artists put into creating those beautiful notes and coins with designs and portraits in varying colors. I was more impressed with the artists' hard work rather than the purchasing power that money had. This was pure human thinking. In fact, even when a single ant died by my hand or foot, I used to feel as if one of my family members had died, because I knew it was family to other ants and was dead due to my mistake. I cursed myself then, thinking that it was such a tiny form of life, how could I kill it? I think when we are born, we are pure humans—a quality which we start losing as we grow up. It does stay alive, however, in a few people, who later try to save this planet from the rest.

We have all the resources to save lives, to combat global warming, to invent new technologies, and yet, we are hindered by money. *We have become so intelligent, yet we are enslaved by systems that prevent us from saving even our own lives when needed. We are hampered by formalities, medical costs, insurance, and other systems that we have created.* Today, it seems as if even when we are dying and need a glass of water before death, we would have to first pay money, after which we can expect a glass of water which may be a full glass or a half, according to the cost. However, if Mother Earth had been a person, she would have fed us the water; she has enough of it and she needs nothing in turn. When are we humans going to learn something from nature? Why, in spite of being so intelligent, do we create our own problems? Why are we stuck in our own systems even when we know what is right and what is the most important thing to do and when? Why do we put up barriers to our own success? These are all the questions that man needs to consider—not just to answer, but to solve them in time, so we can become human beings who value humanity and mankind, all lives, and biodiversity above our belief, systems and material possessions on earth.

We need to breakthrough our worthless systems and protocols or rebuild them unless they stop taking lives of the people or other innocent species of this world.

Earn blessings instead of money, and possess a good character instead of pursuing fame.

Every producer and consumer of money must know that everything on *this planet belongs to each life form that ever lived here in the past, is living in the present, and shall live here in the future.* We alone are not the decision makers on behalf of this entire planet and all living species of creatures on it, for our own purposes. We have no right to make decisions on our own concerning who should live and who should die, who should eat and who should be in hunger, who should get medicines and who should suffer in pain and misery, because everyone on this planet has the right to use its resources and live here without being dominated by anyone else.

We can never produce food from our own bodies; it is the plants and trees that produce the food for us without taking a penny. Then why should any human have to pay for what is already available on earth? We should always concentrate on how we can get ahead by helping each other, sharing the resources, caring for each other, and working together. But look where we are stuck today with so many problems everywhere! We have created our own problems, and now we are struggling to get rid of them without paying attention to what has brought these problems into existence in the first place. If we remove their causes, the problems will be gone, without us wasting our time in solving them.

Today, on the internet, you can purchase land on planet Mars! Who gave us ownership of that entire planet? It has not been that long since we stepped out of earth and now we have started making deals on the entire solar system! I ask everyone, who created it? Did I create it or did you, or the people at NASA, or the ones who sit in the government, or the United Nations? In fact, no one has the right to any other planet on this entire universe, except to this earth on which we were born. If we exceed nature's limitations, nature has its way of putting us back in place. Nature has given us the freedom to explore this universe, to discover, to wonder, and to learn new things that we do not know and have never seen, but it has never given us the right to consider this universe as our property and start profiting from it like a new business.

If we try to dominate everywhere, then the day isn't far off when history will repeat once more—to remind us of every other powerful species that once ruled the earth and are now extinct forever. I guess, in one way or the other, we are more or less heading towards the same destiny. Let us just perish rather than changing ourselves, improving our thoughts and rectifying our mistakes.

We have actually reached a certain place in our lives where we cannot even regret or be sorry for what we have done and are continuing to do, because that list never ends. Even if we do, that is in no way going to compensate for the losses that our own planet has suffered over time. This is the reason that has made me regret why we were born. The earth would have been much better off without the human race. In fact, some other species would have evolved. They may have created a bad impact as well, but it could never have been this bad as it is today, with the existence of human beings. *Our Mother Earth has seen her worst days just because she gave birth to human beings who later turned into monsters and started destroying their own mother to feed their greed.* Even if some of us have not contributed to any of the harmful activities carried out by humans, we are still responsible for what has been happening, and for what happens next, because we didn't stop the ones who lost their extraordinarily intelligent minds and forgot what is right and what is wrong. We need to guide them to the right path. Don't we?

Moving forward, things will need to change. After realizing what harm we have been doing, knowingly or unknowingly, to this planet, its biodiversity and its heritage, let us pledge to make a global and massive change. We may have been the worst species on this planet till today, but from here on let's make a promise to do everything we can to preserve our planet as the most beautiful home in the universe. We understand that with this new goal, we may face armies of enemies, but we will not withdraw from the battle. *We shall prove ourselves brave enough to fight for our mother who has been fighting for centuries against deadly forces to save our lives at the cost of her own.* Let's promise to give earth a better life than what she has had until now. We will kill the monsters that live within us before they destroy it all. This gives us a new goal. And with this, emerges new dreams, a hope, need, and a commitment for a better planet, a clean life, a safe future—that of a good human being. Preserving this planet is preserving *humanity*—that is the most valuable thing we can learn in life.

Stop being possessive and destructive.
All we need to be is constructive and conservative.
Let money be money and not "everything".
And always remember, if there is no one to purchase,
there will be no one selling.

Wealth is not what we own as money, gold, or other material possessions. Real wealth is love, respect, care, happiness, life, family, living beings, earth and its precious biodiversity, etc. The best thing is—they are priceless!

Money has been more a curse than a boon to this entire planet and all its inhabitants. It is up to us to realize our faults and decide for how long we want to be stuck in our own system before we reach the end of our lives. We are inventors, our systems need to change and be more beneficial and useful than harmful and as inefficient as they have been.

To save anything, we think we need money that we have created. However, it cannot save anyone. It is up to us to save everything.

Considering the Impact: Measures to Take

To prevent something from happening, we need to root out the causes that make it happen. To remedy what has already been affected, tools and processes that tackle or diminish the impact need to be introduced. This applies fairly well to global warming and climate change. We obviously need to root out everything that is causing global warming directly or indirectly, and then, at the same time, we also need to involve everything that can reduce or end the impact of global warming like trees for example, that absorb carbon dioxide as well as incoming sun rays, which ultimately help in reducing the impact of global warming by minimizing the greenhouse effect.

The causes of global warming are mainly **greenhouse gases** such as carbon dioxide and methane. These are gaseous elements and so there must be sources that have been continuously emitting these gases into the atmosphere. Our foremost step must be to **remove as many sources of these gases as possible**. Primarily, all living organisms, except green plants and trees (during photosynthesis), release carbon dioxide into the atmosphere as a result of the respiration process. These sources have been there right from the beginning of life on earth but there has never been so much global warming within such a short period of time as has been happening over the past few decades. For tackling that much of carbon dioxide, there has always been a sufficient amount of greenery (forest) that consumes it and releases oxygen into the atmosphere, maintaining a perfect balance in the ecosystem.

But, as the human-race progressed, we introduced more artificial sources of carbon dioxide into the ecosystem than were ever there on this planet. We started burning coal and oil that emitted a huge amount of these greenhouse gases daily into the atmosphere. At the same time, we also started clearing the forests that helped remove those gases from the atmosphere, foolishly removing the very thing that was actually tackling it. This way, the concentration of these gases got so high that today we are facing global warming, causing an impact on global climate, which in turn is affecting all life forms on earth including us.

We need to either stop the heavy sources of greenhouse gases or just use alternatives that do not emit any such gases in anyway. We need to **put** *a stop to the use of coal and petroleum* products such as gasoline/petrol, diesel, kerosene, and even liquefied petroleum gas (LPG). Remember, anything that burns carbon in the presence of air releases carbon dioxide into the atmosphere. Even natural gas (CNG) which is methane, when burned, releases carbon dioxide. Now you may be thinking: Oh my God where do I go now? But remember, *there is always a way to solve everything only when we start seeking it out*. So look for the ways that help stop these sources from being used.

> *"If you always put limits on everything you do, physical or anything else, it will spread into your work and into your life. There are no limits. There are only plateaus, and you must not stay there, you must go beyond them."*
>
> *– Bruce Lee*

Below are some of those hundreds of ways by which you can reduce your carbon footprint and help save the environment from the danger it is in due to us. You can always find a handful of ways on the internet too.

1) **Travel by foot or go on a bicycle** rather than using a fuel-driven vehicle whenever you need to go to a nearby place. Or, if you really care about the environment and the rising danger, you can mostly use your bicycle to go to your office or any other place. There is no such thing as your reputation being tarnished when you are on a bicycle rather than in a Mercedes. You are saving this planet, and hence everybody's life, including your own. And saving life is the greatest act! **Make use of carpooling and public transport** whenever possible. **Take the shortest routes** to your destinations. Electric cars and other vehicles are already on the market. You may always consider purchasing and using a clean-energy vehicle instead of a fossil fuel-driven one.

2) Develop a habit of **turning all unused electrical appliances off**! You need to use as little energy as possible. Especially when no one is using it, you must turn it off. Try not to use an appliance when you can live without it or don't really need it—hair dryers, geysers, air conditioners, room heaters, refrigerators, etc. Do not keep mobile and laptop chargers plugged in all the time or lights and fans on throughout the day and night even when you do not actually need them. Do not keep the music on all the time. Remember, it is an addiction, not a need.

3) **Change all the regular incandescent light bulbs to either CFLs or LEDs**. Also use appliances that help save energy or use less energy and hence bring down your monthly bills. **Do not use an unnecessary number of light bulbs** in shops, showrooms, houses, etc. If you have them, please keep most of them switched off. This means do not use anything more than what you actually need.

4) **Reduce your consumption; reuse as many times as possible**, and **recycle everything that can be**, instead of discarding rampantly and polluting the environment. Never burn garbage because it releases a huge amount of carbon dioxide, and also pollutes the land. Recycle all metals, plastics, paper, rubber, etc. by collecting them daily in separate dustbins and sending them to nearby recycling plants. People can raise the need for recycling plants so that the local corporations, private companies or government help build one in your city. Send all organic waste, like vegetable and food matter, to waste disposal facilities or dispose of it yourself by putting everything in a pit and covering it with soil. Do not throw away the water that is used to wash vegetables and fruits, use it to water plants and trees instead. Always try to reuse everything as many times as possible.

5) **Do not cut or burn trees** and bushes, as burning them will release a huge amount of carbon dioxide, stored within them, into the atmosphere causing a further increment in overall global warming. Do your best to prevent wildfires, because the amount of carbon dioxide released during wildfires within hours is far more than what is released by an entire country within a year.

6) Make partial forest areas denser by **planting more trees**. Or, if you are lazy, then just sprinkle the seeds of the fruits and vegetables on open lands covered with soil whenever the area is wet with water. Plant one or more trees besides your house for your family. It will purify the air, obstruct noise, and cool the surrounding environment.

7) **Regularly service** (clean) **all your machines,** from cars and bikes to fans, air conditioners, furnaces, tires (check if they are properly inflated), etc. so that they consume less electricity and oil. But be sure not to waste water while cleaning; servicing doesn't mean you need to polish the outer surface of your car's body!

8) **Stop burning coal** and stop others too if you see them doing it, by making them aware that they are putting everyone in danger, including themselves, by doing that.

9) **Use kitchen cloths** instead of paper towels, **handkerchiefs** instead of tissue papers, and use **cloth bags** instead of paper or plastic bags for vegetables, groceries, and shopping. Use your **Tiffin box** or **Tupperware** to eat your food on instead of using paper plates.

10) **Wash your clothes by hand** instead of turning on the washing machine every time. And **dry your clothes in the sunlight** instead of using a dryer.

11) **Harvest rain water** during rains. Every house and every apartment must have facilities for rain water harvesting to ensure that maximum water is saved when available and used wisely when needed.

12) **Use** solar water pumps, solar cookers, solar inverters and **solar power** in your homes. Companies are trying to make them cheaper as time goes by. This is the best step towards saving coal and stopping contribution to global warming. Wind power is also a viable option if it is available in your area.

13) Try to **go by stairs instead of using a Lift every time** you need to go up a floor in a building or apartment. And especially, you must not use it when coming down. Don't always consider that you need to use it because you make a monthly payment for it. This reasoning makes you look like you are saying you have paid to cause damage to the environment and so you have the right to do it. Using stairs to go up is an exercise to be fit and healthy in life. The more "short-cuts" we get, the lazier we become. That is what happens most of the time with us.

14) **Eat less meat** and move more towards vegetarianism. There are many reasons behind this, the most essential being that in order to bring meat into the market, more and more bulls, cows, heifers, steers, pigs, goats, etc. are bred and raised so as to meet the increasing demand. These animals release a huge amount of methane into the atmosphere. 28% of greenhouse gasses come from eating meat and from raising cattle. Moreover, non-vegetarians are 40% more likely to be attacked by cancer than vegetarians, because of meat consumption. It is also regarded as cruelty to animals because we feed them and later kill them so that we can eat their meat.

"I'm slowly getting off meat, and I tell you: I feel fantastic."

– Arnold Schwarzenegger

15) **Control your population** in your family and hence in the world. Don't increase unnecessary pressure on the available resources otherwise nobody will be able to survive.

16) **Encourage paying carbon tax** because when you start paying carbon tax, you discourage people and companies from causing pollution involving greenhouse gases mainly carbon dioxide, since the more carbon dioxide they release into the atmosphere, the heavier the tax will be on their pockets. This will also prevent us from making any contribution to the global warming, and ensure a better life ahead. The money collected in tax is used to combat the climate change and offset the other effects of greenhouse gases.

17) **Spread awareness** by encouraging others to conserve the environment. You can all do this by educating people about global warming and its attendant complications and how to stop it by following a few simple steps in life. Or, you can simply gift this book to your family and friends. This will help in spreading awareness as well as raising funds for organizations that are continuously working hard to combat global warming and related issues that we otherwise could not do on our own.

18) **Support the global network of environment and animal welfare organizations** that have been working to conserve the environment and wildlife long before the rest of us developed an awareness of these issues. Their history is quite inspiring and their list of achievements can be viewed on their websites if you want to check them out. So instead of going to a party or going for the same movie again, you can donate the money to these organizations. Believe me; money is more important to them than anything entertaining or luxurious we are going to use it for. Overall, saving this planet is more essential than our enjoyment or entertainment. In fact, every one of us should donate on a monthly basis, whatever we can from our side, considering the amount as compensation for the harm that we might have caused directly or indirectly to the environment, and for conserving this planet and its precious biodiversity.

When you do something good, you really start feeling good and pleasant from within.

Where is the Problem,
and Where Lies the Hope?

Firstly, we need to know the difference between a "need" and a "desire". Anything without which we cannot live or survive is a *need*. Anything without which our life is possible on earth is obviously a *desire*. Earlier, I knew there were three basic needs of humans—food, clothing, and shelter. But now I see, there have appeared many advanced needs of humans, like smart phones, tabs, headphones, GPS, PlayStation, jewelry, etc. I don't understand how these things have become *needs* for the survival of human race; that people say, "Oh God I just can't live without music plugged into my ears". Well, I don't see any polar bears or zebras using GPS to navigate, using cell phones to contact each other, or using smart phones to click group photos. They can do most of these things by themselves naturally. So please, do not call your desires, "needs", because we all know what exactly is needed for the survival of human race on earth but we are going way beyond that. This way, our desires will one day destroy everything that we actually need to live, and that realization will come too late in the day. So *don't let your desires grow into your needs or greed; always try living without them as far as possible*.

I remember a very good story named the "Dragon Ball"—yes, you got it right, the cartoon series that aired on TV. The story was all about dragon balls that people relied on. To solve their troubles, they summoned the eternal dragon out of those dragon balls to grant their wishes. Initially, people used this to solve their bigger problems. But, eventually, they started relying heavily on them and each time they needed to solve a problem, however small, they would just summon the dragon to solve everything through the granting of wishes. Each time, the dragon balls were used, the negative energy inside them increased to a certain specific level. Then, one day, when the negative energy reached its maximum, a completely evil dragon emerged that granted no more wishes; rather it brought poison, death, and misery to all life forms on earth. People later questioned why they needed dragon balls. The catastrophe had happened because *they had relied too much on them to solve all their problems in life rather than engaging themselves in finding other solutions.*

The story of our life is going down a similar path. We are relying heavily on coal and petroleum without caring about their increasing negative impact on the environment which is, in this case, abnormal increase in the levels of carbon dioxide and methane in the atmosphere. When this negative energy reaches its maximum, the earth is surely going to be in danger, as well as all life on it. Hence, before that happens, we need to stop relying on these resources to fulfill our requirements. We should, rather, use alternatives that do not cause any harm to the environment in the longer run.

Well, we understand that switching over to alternate sources and stopping the use of coal and petroleum is not so easy. However, for power (electricity), *we can use renewable sources like solar, wind or hydro power,* and also transform transportation services by introducing electric cars, solar-powered planes, electric boats, etc. but we still lack these technologies for regular use. This is because they cannot yet sustain the levels of productivity that we are currently used to, specifically those that are derived from fuel-driven vehicles or coal-powered systems, which is one of the primary reasons why we haven't switched over to renewable energy alternatives yet. Other reasons are their limited availability and high costs which discourage people from opting for them. What we have got to actually do is make those technologies reliable enough to meet our daily needs. Only then people will be ready to switch over to clean and green energy solutions that cause 0% pollution in the environment.

"The future is green energy, sustainability, renewable energy."

– Arnold Schwarzenegger

And one such *clean and reliable source of energy is hydrogen*. Yes, hydrogen is not available abundantly on earth in its native form but is present in large amounts in water, which occupies more than 70% of earth's surface. Hydrogen can be extracted from water without using any chemicals, i.e. simply by using the process of electrolysis where electricity is used to break down water molecules into their components – hydrogen and oxygen. Where hydrogen (as compressed gas or liquefied) can be stored for use as fuel in transportation systems like cars, buses, planes, ships, etc. and also to produce electricity (fuel cells and others), the oxygen (as compressed gas or liquefied) can also be stored to be used in hospitals, space, sea diving, etc. or simply released into the atmosphere. And all the electricity required to carry on the process of electrolysis can be harnessed from the sun using solar panels. So where there is water, there is fuel, and hence energy.

Think of hydrogen extraction plants in place of crude oil plants or coal mines/extraction plants. Extraction of hydrogen involves no damage to the environment as in the case of crude oil or coal. The same processes can be carried on here—transporting the hydrogen to hydrogen centers instead of petrol pumps for use in vehicles on roads. Burning of hydrogen creates water which is so pure that even if we drink it, there will be no harm at all. I hope you remember the car from the innovative company "Honda" that expelled water from its exhaust; that was the car running on hydrogen. This energy is one of the cleanliest on earth with no harmful byproduct. Everything in this entire process is useful and eco-friendly.

"The mind is the limit. As long as the mind can envision the fact that you can do something, you can do it, as long as you really believe 100 percent."

– Arnold Schwarzenegger

Electrolysis of water *is the decomposition of water (H_2O) into* **oxygen** *(O_2) and* **hydrogen** *gas (H_2) due to an electric current being passed through the water. The reaction has a standard potential of -1.23 V, meaning it ideally requires a potential difference of 1.23 volts to split water.*

Although the handling of hydrogen is not as easy as we think, yet it is a worthwhile solution for our scientists to work on. What is needed on our part is to acknowledge the change that they make. These technologies are in their beginning stage and require our support to become fully functional. They need financial support as well as our acceptance and willingness to integrate them into our lives when they are available. In this, the government plays a key role. Hence, the government has to be the first body to bring these new technologies to work. They need to support these developments so that we can together combat global warming by completely eliminating the use of fossil fuels as sources of energy. And the government will support these developments once we, the people, make a demand and voice our concern on how important they really are.

"We are a forward-looking people, and we must have a forward-looking government."

– Arnold Schwarzenegger

In the meantime, we can also *focus largely on stopping deforestation while pursuing afforestation simultaneously*. Afforestation is the planting of trees and expanding the green cover. Forests not only help in removing carbon dioxide from the atmosphere, but also purify the air and bring rainfall. They also add to the scenic beauty of the environment. But companies keep on felling more and more trees to fulfill our needs, which are actually not our needs but simply, addictions. Products ranging from margarine and chocolate to ice creams, soaps, cosmetics, and fuel for cars and power plants, involve the use of palm oil as an ingredient. Palm oil plantations need less than half the land required by other crops to produce the same amount of oil which makes it the least expensive vegetable oil in the world. Palm oil plantations result in the clear cutting of tropical hardwoods, the killing of local wildlife, the displacement of local communities, and a significant increase in greenhouse gas emissions. So if we stop using these products and demand a ban on palm oil, the companies engaging in harmful activities will be highly discouraged from carrying on such activities, as well as deforestation, in the name of fulfilling our desires. *We need to keep ourselves informed about which company is bringing us the products we use and at what cost, because the cost can be anything from deforestation to people's slavery, misuse of animals, loss of their habitat, etc., which cannot be compensated for by the money we pay for such products.* So while choosing products for your daily use, do not forget to investigate what they are made of and how the ingredients are acquired. They cannot carry on businesses that involve harming the environment if we don't buy their products; it is as simple as that. This will force them to stop using palm oil that results in deforestation and people's slavery.

It is not enough for us to let our Mother Earth survive but *live*, like she once did, in full glory, when we were in her womb. How do we forget the one who gave us birth, fed us everything we ever wanted, and supported our life to be where we are today, while, we are entrenched on a path of killing her. Our Mother Earth is dying slowly and surely from within. She sees that no one cares for her. She has always done everything in her reach to save our lives, to make it better, but now, her body has gone weaker than has ever been in her whole life—because she has always wanted good for us. Yet we simply exploit her and will continue doing so until her death. We don't deserve to be even called "humans" anymore. We're considered the most intelligent creatures on earth. This intelligence has blinded us in a way which doesn't let us foresee our ruined future. It only promises us more technology and luxuries that exploit the earth. We are building our future at the cost of the planet on which we live. What answer will we give to future generations on where we were or what we were doing when we needed to take action to save this planet, its biodiversity, and its heritage? We will certainly be the ones responsible for turning their bright future into chaos and disaster.

Environmental leaders have stepped forward, working hard to make positive changes happen. But the reality is they cannot do it alone. They need our help to save our lives, our future, this planet, and the generations ahead. They create new policies, new rules, invent new technologies, promote renewable energy solutions, encouraging us to switch to something which we are not used to but we need to if we really want a good future with a safe planet. However, we will not see that change happen until we take action and adopt those policies; until we switch to renewable energy solutions and stop using fossil fuels; until we stop causing deforestation and forest fires; until we stop polluting the air, water and land; until we are genuinely concerned that our planet is dying; until we take up the responsibility of making change really happen. Yes, we can make this work. So far, their suggestions have found no traction as we have been sitting idly in the comfort of our homes and offices without actually considering what they have been recommending us to do, or making changes in our lifestyle and incorporating those ideas that make a better and safer planet.

> *"Just remember, you can't climb the ladder of success with your hands in your pockets."*
>
> *– Arnold Schwarzenegger*

We do not need to fret for what we do not have or can't do. Instead, *we need to focus on what we can do with whatever means we have available to us*. Do you think only a rich child can help his/her mother and a child who has nothing cannot do anything? If you think so, then you need to open up your mind and look at the most precious thing God has given you—your life. *It will be an honour to sacrifice our lives to save our planet, in return for what she has been sacrificing for the life of the entire human race*.

"Why should I when others do not?" Or, "I will only do if they do, otherwise not". It is because "they" are thinking the same way as you:

why should they do anything if you do not, or they will only do if you do, otherwise not. If you are one of those who thinks this way, then it's time you switch your thinking the other way around and be the first to take action, instead of waiting for others to take the initiative.

Remember that others are waiting for you to start—you do not have the luxury of waiting for others to take the lead until everything gets out of control. Always think, you are the leader and you will show others the right way to go. Be the first to do something good. Be the first to take action. Be the first to start the movement. Be the first to step up for the good of mankind. Your actions will inspire everyone to do what you have been expecting others to do. Then the same question will be reversed for the rest: why shouldn't I do if everyone else has started doing it? The most important thing is to get started. *It is our actions today that determine our future, where we will be tomorrow.*

Raise your voice, stand for your cause, and take the right action at the right time. Let people learn from you...if you can do it all alone, then why can't they? You are doing this for your life, for your family, for your planet and you don't need anybody's permission to save your mother who is keeping you alive. When she has done everything she can to sustain us then it is an honour to have the opportunity to do something for her. She has been serving us since the beginning of the human race without getting anything in return. *What she really needs is our love, our dedication, our care, and our support to get back to normal again.* Let us show what we as her children can do on our part for our mother.

We cannot recover what we have lost, no matter how much we regret whatever wrong we've done for the whole of our life. No life lost in accidents, murders, wars, and disasters can be brought back ever again. But, as long as we are alive, we always have the chance to make up for our mistakes, even now. The first step is realizing what wrong we did or are still doing. Only after which, can we be up for doing something good and promise to ourselves not to repeat the same mistakes again. Opportunity often finds us. In fact, it is often waiting for us to realize our mistakes and come forward to put everything back the way it should be in nature. As humans, we can do our best. It is time that will reveal whether we are successful or not. So always consider doing whatever you can without waiting for the results. When you're done, take a long breath, have a look back at where you started, and compare it to where you are now. You will then know what has changed and how much of your efforts have actually contributed to restore harmony and balance to nature as well as generate development and progress throughout the world.

Remember, *you decide your own journey of life. Leave your footprints behind so that the world will know the right way to go when they are lost.*

"The key to immortality is first living a life worth remembering."

– Bruce Lee

I believe that people should commit themselves to achieving the goal of saving the life of this dying planet before we are all gone, and to let coming generations know how we dealt with the most sophisticated problems ever in the history of mankind and planet earth, indeed, created by us, but successfully solved in time, before it was too late. This is how we are going to shape the entire future. This is how we teach and inspire others to decide wisely between what is right and what is wrong. This is how we set everything back to normal once again and improve our lives. This is how we are going to live once again, like we did before, happily, with our ever-caring Mother Earth. This is how everything is going to change. And this is how we are going to be this change. And so be it!

In fact, every single one of us can help save the life of our planet. It is time for action. It is time when children teach their parents or grandparents how simply lighting a light bulb when not required is contributing to the entire climate change that we may not see but is taking place all over the planet and causing devastation on a global scale. It is time to know and understand that what we have been considering insignificant issues may have vast repercussion threatening our planet's life. Be a good human. Love, care and respect nature. *Be good and caring children of a mother—our planet earth.*

Love and respect for nature and animals needs be inculcated right from the beginning of one's life. Hence, we need to inculcate this character in our children right from the beginning of their life so that as they grow, they will never think of harming the environment and will always understand the importance of conservation in their lives.

Q. What do I get when I do anything for the environment or for this planet?

- The air (primarily oxygen) you are breathing in comes from the environment. If you think you can survive without breathing, then give it a try and you will know whether you really need it.

- The food and water that you consume every day comes directly and indirectly from the environment.

- The clothes that you put on also come from the environment.

- The materials used in building your beautiful dream home come from the environment.

- The place you live in or the school or office you go to, all lie within the environment.

The list goes on…

And the environment lies on this planet earth.

Your life would be completely void without this environment. We all need it. In fact, we all enjoy its benefits. But when we are asked to do something for the environment, we start making excuses, preferring to play a sport or go to a party. Consider, if the planet had the same attitude about supplying everything (mainly air, water, and food) to us! If it stops supplying oxygen, even for a minute, we will all start suffocating and will be on our knees begging nature for a second chance.

Greenery – The Home of Life

Trees, a major part of this earth, are the lungs of our Mother Earth, which take in carbon dioxide and release oxygen—the next precious element after water which supports our life as well as the lives of all those millions and billions of creatures which live on earth. These plants and trees are living. They don't have families like us but they are much like other species of this world. They don't talk, laugh, cry or have emotions like joy, grief, etc. but they have a sense of feeling which is "hurt". Yes, they get hurt when they are cut, burned, or are subjected to vigorous damage.

Greenery — The Colour of Life

Trees support the lives of almost all the living species of this world. Not only this, but they also provide fruits and vegetables to all organisms surviving on land directly or indirectly, including human beings and many aquatic organisms. They provide us with food, the next most precious thing after oxygen, that we need for survival. And another amazing fact you must know about them is that they also provide us with fresh and pure water (the most precious element of all) indirectly, through transpiration (loss of water through the surfaces of leaves). They absorb water from underground sources through their roots and expel it out of their leaves as water vapour, which eventually assists in the formation of heavy clouds and finally manifests as rain. Plants consume only 2% of the water which they take in from the ground and the rest is given back to the environment. Hence, trees are responsible for rainfall. Where there are more trees, there is more rainfall; where there are fewer trees, there is less rainfall and where there are no trees, there is hardly any rainfall, and such places are obviously deserts that receive extremely less rainfall in comparison to other parts of this world.

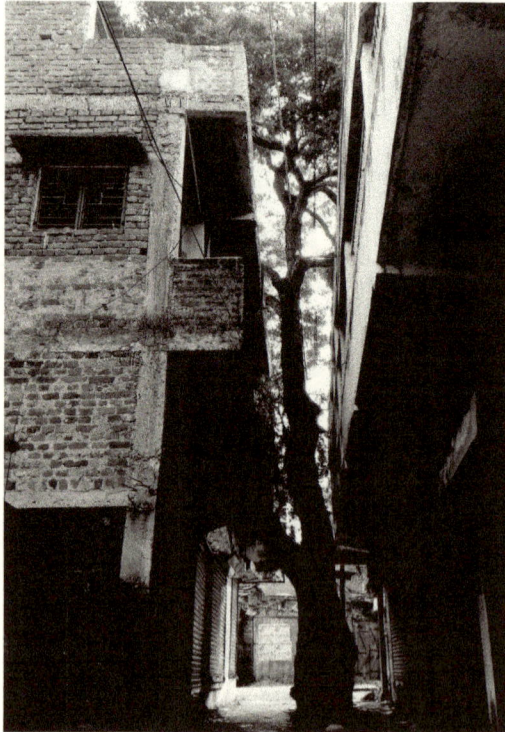

A Tree struggling between Houses

Do you know?

While trees do bring rainfall, they also protect us against the storms which are harmful to our life and property. Plants and trees are also the source of various medicines which we use to cure different kinds of diseases. They also purify the air that we breathe by removing dust particles, diseases, and harmful gases. So if we take a moment to pause and think about them, we will realize that trees do a lot of things for the environment and for us. But it is what human beings do that is really a matter to be concerned about. They are cutting down trees indiscriminately, to fulfill their own needs for buildings, furniture, beds, houses, vehicles, etc. They have now become so blind that to fulfill their desires, they are destroying the very sources that supply their needs.

* *Desire – Those things without which man can survive.*
* *Need – Those things without which man cannot survive.*

A Mother, which stands to support our life.

Man should understand that trees don't meet his needs alone, but also the needs of all the living species of this world. So he cannot take it upon himself to destroy trees for his own selfish needs and desires. Trees, which have been supporting our existence since our first footstep on earth, are now gifted 'Death' from our side. Is this what we have learned over the course of our whole life—to destroy the ones that protect us? This is the "gift" man has given to trees and vegetation for supporting his life for thousands of years.

It took over 20 years for some, 60 for others, sometimes even more than 150 years for trees to grow and forests to form, surviving hot summers, floods, storms, and chilling winters.

But how long does it take us to cut them down, back to the ground from where they began the journey of life?

Whether as a home to thousands of animals or a source of food for the rest, they stand up for us all. It takes almost an entire human lifetime to see a tree grow from a tiny seedling to its full mighty form. Sometimes, it takes even generations for them to reach their full height. They add to the beauty of this planet. They are the source of freshness, completeness, serenity, and most importantly—life.

We cut them, burn them, uproot them, but this is not the end.

They stand up once again, for you, for me, for all the species on this planet to which they have ever served a home, a source of food, and lungs to all life. No matter how many times you betray your mother, she still comes back for one and only reason—to support your life, so that you live forever.

So before you cut down a tree, take a moment to consider the length of time it has taken to become what you see it as today, which may have been more than your overall lifespan. How much it must have endured to reach this stage where it can support so many lives, including its own.

A tree belongs to such a species which is looked after by nature when it is a small plant, and when it grows mature, it cares for itself. It is an autotroph (produces its own food), so it is a self-dependent organism. They support our lives in numerous ways:

1) They supply us with oxygen.

2) Provide food—fruits, nuts, vegetables, etc.

3) Provide water in the form of rainfall (indirectly).

4) Protect against storms.

5) Provide medicines—Ayurvedic (directly) and Non-Ayurvedic (indirectly).

6) Purify the air by removing dust particles, diseases, and toxic gases.

7) Prevent soil erosion by holding soil particles together with their roots.

8) Cool the environment by absorbing most of the sun rays.

9) Supply us with valuable materials for the manufacture of coir, rubber, ropes, chocolate, sugar, honey (indirectly) and many more, for industrial and domestic uses.

10) Reduce noise pollution by absorbing sound waves.

11) Prevent the spread of diseases.

12) Prevent global warming by resisting greenhouse effect—absorbing sun rays and carbon dioxide (the main cause).

13) Provide food and shelter to animals.

14) Center of attraction for thousands of amazing, incredible, and beautiful birds, butterflies, bees, and other animals.

15) Lastly, they contribute to the natural scenic beauty of the environment— inspiring generations of poets and artists.

Trees have made our life possible on earth for thousands of years, and hence we should be indebted to them forever. So, if we get an opportunity to serve them then we should consider it a privilege and step forward with a pure heart to care for the ones which have been caring for us since our first step on earth.

Trees are to be treated like our mothers.

They are to be loved, cared for, and respected not only by us but all the other species of this world. The fact is that the other species do care, but we are the species that tend to forget most often.

Things to do:

Nothing impossible, just these few steps to be followed strictly:

1) We all must **plant at least one tree on our birthday every year** as a gift to Mother Nature for our successful life on earth. Now our work doesn't end just by planting a tree. We also need to care for it till it grows mature and becomes self-dependent.

2) We must **write completely on every page** of our notebooks. No pages or part of the pages must be left blank. Paper must not be wasted.

3) **Rather than purchasing new books every time**, we must try to **get the used books** from our elders or friends for our use. This will cause a decrease in the demand for new books and hence prevent further felling of trees for the manufacturing of paper that is used to create new books. And, as far as possible, all the companies manufacturing paper products—such as books, newspapers, etc. must **use recycled papers** instead of new ones to manufacture their products. We should **opt for eBooks** (electronic books) whenever possible, instead of purchasing paperback editions.

4) We must **recycle paper** instead of burning or throwing them out as garbage. We should send used paper to paper recycling companies for recycling, where old and used papers are converted into completely new ones to be used once again by processing them through a series of chemical processes.

5) We must try to **wish our friends and relatives verbally** (or digitally) on occasions such as Birthday, Marriage, New Year, Marriage Anniversary, etc. and also invite them on our occasions personally instead of using greetings cards, birthday cards, marriage cards, anniversary cards, and other sorts of invitation cards printed on paper.

6) We must try to **use less wooden furniture** and decrease the demand for such products consequently. Instead, we can use furniture made of other environment-friendly synthetic materials.

7) **Shifting cultivation must be strictly prohibited.** In this system, a part of forest land is cleared and is used for cultivation till it is fertile. The land is left barren when it becomes infertile and farmers move on to other forest lands. In this way, both lands and vegetation get destroyed on a large scale.

8) **Trees must be planted on crop lands** in between different sections of crops. This will help in preventing soil erosion and would thus retain the fertility of the soil for the growth of healthier crops.

9) Hospitals, public libraries, houses, and hotels must be **surrounded by vegetation** to prevent noise pollution. The presence of vegetation obstructs the flow of sound waves, and hence people in houses, public libraries, hotels, and patients in hospitals, can work, study, sleep, and recover peacefully.

10) We **must not unnecessarily break the twigs and branches** of a tree. They are very precious because each set of leaves is responsible for balancing the level of carbon dioxide released by living organisms including us. We should not unnecessarily disturb this balance.

11) **Discourage companies** who create products through felling trees or clearing forest lands.

12) When we cut down a tree, according to a study, we must **plant at least ten plant saplings** to compensate for the loss. This is a rule that has been framed for both the common man as well as industrialists, by the government, regarding environmental concern.

13) All **barren and empty lands must be covered with green trees and vegetation** as far as possible. This will help reduce the amount of sun rays reflected back into the atmosphere, and also reduce carbon dioxide from the atmosphere. This could double our efforts in the attack on global warming.

14) **Protect the trees and forest areas** whenever you learn that somebody is about to clear the forest areas or cut down even a single tree. We must always defend the trees that help to sustain our life on earth.

A tree—is not just a huge piece of wood, covered with green leaves and colourful flowers sprouting from its thick branches and thinner twigs. It offers shade, under which flourishes life of all the other species of this world. It's a Mother. Worship it, love it, pray for it, and help it grow. By doing this, you support your own life as well as others.

We need to care for the one who supports our life.

In the year 2009, renowned filmmaker, director and producer James Cameron released his highest ever grossing movie – Avatar. Do you remember the magnificent environment, the forest or jungle, or the animals? All those were created using real world references available on earth combined with artists' creative imaginations. That beauty already exists here on earth which James Cameron and his team had envisioned in the movie for the planet Pandora. The thing is if you do not know anything about nature then how would you create it so beautifully? Our earth has enough unbelievably beautiful natural creations to keep you amazed your entire life. Beauty of Nature is far beyond our explanation—it is incredible and precious, hence we should preserve it before it is all gone from our planet.

Animals – The Invaluable Forms of Life

Most of the species in this world, besides human beings, belong to the Animal Kingdom. They are beautiful, amazing, and incredible creations of nature. We have been fortunate to live with them for centuries, but we may soon lose this opportunity if we do not become mindful of the ways they are suffering, and that some are even becoming extinct. We have been engaging animals in work since primitive times. Since man appeared on earth, he lived side by side with animals, sharing their food and working together. They contributed to the progress of Mankind when we were in need, and now it's our turn to do something for them. They need us..

Animals are extremely important to us and to the environment. Besides greenery, animals are the ones who, along with us, contribute to making our environment a thriving ecosystem. They are important to us and the environment in many ways:

(i) **Maintain Balance in the Ecosystem** – The most important reason for the existence of all living organisms, including human beings, is to maintain a balance in the ecosystem. This balance is achieved through the food chain. All organisms occupy certain positions in the food chain. A food chain is that medium through which energy is transferred from one living organism to the other. The transfer of food energy from the producers (green plants), through a series of organisms – herbivores (plant-eating organisms) to carnivores (flesh–eating organisms) to decomposers (bacteria and fungi) with constant eating and being eaten is known as food chain. A typical terrestrial food chain may be as follows: - Green plants > Mouse > Snake > Eagle > Decomposers. While an aquatic food chain may be this way: - Algae > Aquatic insects > Small fish > Bigger fish > Birds > Decomposers. Decomposers act on dead bodies and return most of the energy to the soil which green plants re-absorb as minerals and salts. Many food chains are inter-connected with each other to form Food Webs. Food webs are responsible for maintaining the balance in biological environment. For example, a decrease in the population of rabbits will naturally cause an increase in the population of herbivorous mice. This may decrease the population of carnivores that prefer to eat rabbits. Moreover, a balanced ecosystem is essential for the survival of all the living organisms of the system of which we are also a part.

They have a beautiful family like us.

(ii) **Help us naturally in our works** – We all know that animals have been helping us since our ancestors domesticated them. Dogs, cows, camels, buffaloes, elephants, horses, donkeys, etc. are some of the animals which assist us, mostly in long journeys and travels to remote areas, for protection, as security guards, as guidance to detect dangers, etc. They may also be supporting us in ways we are generally not aware of.

(iii) **Provide us valuable products** – Certain animals provide many valuable materials such as milk, honey, alcohol, curd (by bacteria), etc. that we consume or sell for an income. Bio-gas plants (using mainly cow dung as one of the raw materials) are a good source of renewable energy.

(iv) **Maintain cleanliness in the environment** – When an organism dies, the body of that organism is soon eaten up by carnivores such as hawks, vultures, eagles, hyenas, etc. while the rest of the body is finally broken down by the decomposers—the bacteria and fungi. They decompose the bodily remains into elements which mix with the soil as humus and the rest of the elements may be gaseous which move into the atmosphere. This humus enriches the soil with lots of nutrients making the soil extremely fertile. Fertile soil (lands) gives healthy crops to us in turn. Not only this, the bacteria "Rhizobium" present in the root nodules of the leguminous plants also enrich the soil with nitrogen compounds to make it fertile. Earthworms and ants also do the same thing but in a different way. They dig through the soil, bringing the fertile bottom layer of soil to the top, sending the infertile soil on top, downwards, thus retaining the fertility of the soil. This system also helps to give the germinating seeds of plants and crops access to fresh air and water for their healthy growth.

(v) **Form a subject matter for study and a source of knowledge** – Animals have been a subject matter for our study for decades. We have derived a huge amount of information from animals by observing and studying them, which we are using now in many of our technologies. By observing them, we learn numerous things about their lives and about how they affect our lives and the environment. They are a source of inspiration to us.

(vi) **Other miscellaneous contributions to us and the environment** – Birds consume the flesh of fruits and scatter their seeds here and there which results in the growth of numerous plants and trees. Butterflies and bees are responsible for self and cross pollination in flowers which produce new breeds of flowers and healthy fruits. Small birds and fish eat up the larva of mosquitoes living in the still water of ponds, tanks, etc. In this way, they help in reducing the number of mosquitoes and their spreading. In the same way, lizards, chameleons, frogs etc. consume house flies and other insects which spread various harmful diseases. Thus, these organisms directly or indirectly contribute a lot to the maintenance of our healthy and balanced environment.

There are, undoubtedly, many more contributions about which we know either little or nothing. There are many living species on this planet which haven't yet been discovered, while the ones that have been, are still under observation by zoologists and other scientists. They are trying to acquire as much information and knowledge as possible through their observations and studies.

The most surprising information they discovered during their study was that many animals and other species that they had just begun to research were already on the verge of extinction! They are now wondering how this could happen and what might be the reason behind it. When they broadened the scope of their study, they found that the main reason behind this was one species which is not only the most intelligent on earth, but greedy and mean spirited too. We are talking of none other than the human species to which they themselves belong. The most popular and well-known species of all, whose pain Mother Earth has been enduring for centuries.

Obviously, the sort of activities that we have been carrying out throughout the world is directly or indirectly causing the other species of this world to perish. We have cleared vast tracts of forest lands to build houses, buildings, industries, power plants, resorts, entertainment spots, playgrounds, stadiums, airports, railways, roads, dig out mines, test and detonate heavy explosives, and various sorts of construction and other activities to create extremely happy and comfortable lives for ourselves. But in fulfilling our own means, we knowingly or unknowingly have left nothing for the other innocent species of this world to survive. We have relentlessly destroyed their habitat and their food sources on the way to fulfilling our selfish desires. It never occurred to us that our selfish activities could destroy the lives of other species so badly, that they would be driven to the verge of extinction. They need to survive on this planet and they are continuously struggling to survive even when they don't have their favourable food and shelter (habitat). They have to face thousands of problems and threats every day, but are still trying their best to manage their lives and preserve their species.

Now, if we don't step forward to help them get their environment back, then unfortunately, they are no longer going to be with us on this earth. We need to save them; save their precious lives. They are incredibly important to us and the environment. Absence of any species from this world could lead to a dramatic change in the ecosystem. Environmental changes could be triggered, that may affect our lives and have negative impact not only on us, but also on all other living species of this world. Hence, we need to stop them from falling into the invisible mouth of extinction, where they will be lost forever. Thus, we need to restore their habitat. We have already broken the rules of nature by taking away their food and shelter for our own use. We have no right to do that. We need to improve our way of thinking. We should not play with their lives in our greed and with selfish intentions, because life is the most precious gift of all from God, which once lost, can never be brought back. The value of a life is greater than material possessions. And what are possessions even worth if we prevent animal life from being able to sustain itself, which will ultimately lead to an unsustainable future for humans?

Do you know why so many animals and insects enter our houses and other places stealing food and damaging our property?

It all happens because we, the most intelligent creatures in this world, have tried to prove our superiority by dominating this planet. We have captured the lands and built our own houses on habitats which belonged to animals and insects; therefore, they enter our homes, steal food, destroy our property, and go away only to return the next day. It is not their fault. As they don't have any other available shelter (habitat) or food due to deforestation, they are bound to look for their needs in our homes. They just invade the city-houses, shops, churches, temples, goods storage rooms, restaurants, hotels, garages, etc. in search for food and shelter. They are ready to do anything for food and attack us suddenly and directly, face to face, with no fear. Thus, from all these occurrences, we finally understand how the absence of forest cover affects the lives of animals. We should not try to violate the rules of nature because whenever we try to make such an attempt, nature soon makes us pay for it directly or indirectly with no mercy.

What about selling animals? In fact, how dare we sell animals!? We have reduced them to goods that can be smuggled, traded, or sold like commodities. How can we measure the cost of a life and put a price on it? No living beings should be purchased or sold. If the selling of human beings is a crime, then how can the selling of animals be a legitimate business?

The life contained inside an egg is quite invaluable. It protects the unborn infant of an animal or a bird—that has not even opened its little eyes to take a look at this world where it's just about to begin its life. But how much does it cost us to get that egg and end the life flourishing in it?! Of course, hardly Rs. 5 (in India) or 13 eggs for a dollar, and that too from the humans, and not directly from the animal or bird who actually laid those eggs, and who would never sell their infants in any way, not even for food. But we do it! This sets a very common example: how we've made life a product which can be sold or purchased for a sum of money. We've set a monetary value for life on our own. It's not that we would die if we don't kill an animal to feed our hunger. We are omnivorous. Even when we know how valuable each life on this planet is, still, we destroy it for our means. In fact, we are much more concerned about our own lives! I wonder what we would have done, or how we would have felt, if we were in place of the animals, or the animals would've started a business on selling us doing exactly what we do to them. Whenever I think about it, it feels animals are far better than us in most cases. I consider, if a life inside an egg could cost only around Rs. 5, then our life shouldn't even be costing Rs. 2, because we've already degraded the value of our life by valuing no other lives on this planet. *The value of our life increases only when we learn to value the lives of others, irrespective of the form in which the life embodies.*

Their lives — Our business

Now, even if we come to understand this, there are still many people who choose money over animals. They are unaware that they are choosing money over their own lives. These people, just for a few thousand rupees or dollars, mercilessly kill innocent animals and sell their bones, teeth, skulls, nails, and skins to earn black-market money. They also steal animals from the protected reserves and sanctuaries and later kill them to sell their parts for a fortune. Sometimes, even the security guards of the reserves are involved as they get a share of the illegal profits. So, just for a sum of money, these people play with the lives of the helpless animals. They don't even have any information about the importance of these animals to us and to the environment, since money has made them blind. Most of the time these people are caught by the police and are sentenced to imprisonment for years, while the real culprits behind them, escape. So, who are the real culprits behind these illegal businesses? They are the people who create a demand for these animals' parts as ornaments, aphrodisiacs or luxury clothing and accessories. They buy these garments simply to flaunt their wealth. But what these garments really demonstrate is that the wearers may have excess amounts of money in their hands but lack common sense and a kind heart, which true caring human beings possess irrespective of being rich or poor, black or white, literate or illiterate.

"Showing off is the fool's idea of glory."

– Bruce Lee

Now, the matter doesn't end here. There are also some people who really treat animals in such a way that it denotes they are inhumane and absolutely heartless. They care for neither any people nor animals. They have just appeared in this world to harm others and enjoy watching others in pain. Their attitude towards innocent animals is quite disgusting. They don't kill the animals at once, but they cause them extreme pain and leave them to die slowly over a long period of time.

For example, when I was just a small child, I had a small, cute puppy which lived beside my house. I used to feed him every day, most often accompanied by my mother. But one day, when I was alone at home, there appeared three young children, who, when they noticed the puppy, drove him into a big pit from which he could not emerge. Then, one of those three children brought a solid red brick and threw it on the helpless puppy with all his energy. The puppy whined so loudly that I could hear severe pain in its cry—the kind of pain that could not be endured even for a second. Then the other two boys also did the same thing, i.e., threw brick after brick on the trapped puppy, crushing its little limbs, breaking its ribs and bones into innumerable pieces. Finally, one of the brick pieces cracked its tender skull and they left the puppy to die a painful, unendurable death. God took mercy upon that helpless creature and thus the puppy's life left its body within 15 - 20 minutes after that harsh event. While this was going on, I could do nothing, since I had been locked in from outside. So I could only watch this painful moment through a small hole in the front door of my house. My eyes were flushed with tears, my heart bled for that poor puppy but I could do nothing. I was absolutely helpless to save that innocent animal from cruel inhuman creatures who had appeared straight from hell.

After a while, when my mother returned home from the market, I told her everything that I had witnessed, crying my heart out. Mother reassured me that had she been there she would never have let it happen. The next day, when the mother of that dead puppy arrived at the yard of my house, I didn't know what to tell her. I just sat down on the stairs before her. I had no words to speak. I looked into her eyes and she also looked into mine in turn, and I said, I couldn't save your baby, I'm sorry. She took no action but I could see the tears in her eyes. As a child, I used to call her "Mom"; she loved me very much and was still faithful to me—a human being.

This is just one of several such painful events in my life during childhood. I want to raise a question here: what would the reaction have been if what happened to that puppy had happened to the child of a human being? The mother of that child would have cried and shouted like anything with no self-control; whereas, the dog was also a mother but she didn't make a single sound, not that she did not feel the pain or she had a habit of losing children, instead she knew that she had to face still many more such cases in the future as long as human beings exist on this earth and with that thought, she had to make her heart stronger and further, dare to be a mother once again. This is the way of survival. Moreover, if it had been a human child killed by an animal, then that animal would have been surely killed by the people. Huh! This is the difference between us and the animals. They have a pure heart, not like us—filled with lots of harmful waste products like dominance, greed, jealousy, revenge, etc. Their souls are as pure as heaven which we, unfortunate human beings, can never possess since we have already contaminated our souls with innumerable and unforgivable sins.

I have witnessed many more cases where puppies and kittens or even cats crossing the road are crushed by four wheelers, where the driver didn't even stop for a minute to let them pass. And they are ran over not just once but again and again even after their death i.e., people continue to ride their vehicles right over their dead bodies as if nothing was ever there. Dogs and puppies shiver in winter, sitting outside the gates of houses hoping to be noticed by someone who can spare them some bread—but most of the time they sleep on an empty stomach, without even a drop of water. They have to survive on one piece of bread a day and a handful of sewage water if they find no clean water to drink. Sometimes, they get rotten food to eat, which causes them to vomit. Knowing that they might not get another chunk of food, they eat their vomit. Thus, they become lean—with their ribs, bones, and skull turning more visible in course of time. I know the intensity of their situation is hard for many to believe. But know that they are not alive in their skin; their days are leading them towards a slow, painful death. And why is this even happening? What have they ever done to us that we are making them pay for it in such a terrible way?

Dogs struggling outside in Chilling Winter.

A cow is bleeding on the roadside because somebody has stabbed his forelimb with a rod of steel and it has to walk with that rod still sticking out of his limb and no one stops to help! A dog, running helplessly on the road, is bleeding, because someone has stitched his whole body with a steel wire from stomach to intestines and nobody knows who did it. It wanders near a doctor's clinic and sits outside, but the doctor never comes out to heal him. He dies.

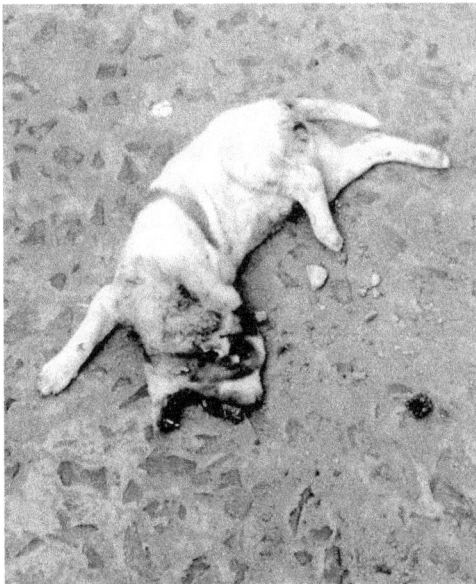

People kept on riding their vehicles over this puppy as if nothing was ever there.

51

Another dog crossing a not-so-busy road gets hit by a truck because the truck driver didn't care to slow down. The dog gets caught under the wheels which crushes its torso and the truck simply keeps going, escaping the situation. The dog cries for help because the fractures are so intense that it is in severe pain, but no one ever comes to help it, as there are no animal hospitals nearby. After it dies, slowly over time, in extreme pain, and bleeding from the mouth, everyone passing through the road maintains a distance from the dead body, covering their noses, exclaiming it to smell so nasty while a few laugh at the way the helpless creature died with its mouth and eyes open.

A goat tied with a rope stands with his eyes wide open in a chevon/mutton shop, where he has to face the chopped heads of his companions. Oh wow, the butcher gives him few twigs with leaves to eat, not so that he feels better before he dies, but so that he weighs more on the weighing scale when the butcher sells his meat. The goat eats no more; he falls absolutely silent for he comes to know that soon his head will be right there on the table beside his companions. Many of them, watching this happening, struggle to get out of the ropes, begging help from every passersby, tugging on their clothes and bleating so loudly that you can hear their cries all over the market, but who helps?

We are all monsters, aren't we? Thinking back on when I was a child, I can't help but wonder how all these situations would have impacted my feelings, and that fills my heart with despair and contempt for humans. After all, why wouldn't it be?! This is not just about me, though. This is about how we are impacting many generations of people, especially the generation after us. What are we teaching them and what are we leaving for them. It all matters. But do enough of us realize that and do we really care?

Harming and killing the animals for self-use,
profit or entertainment and fun is generally
termed as Cruelty to Animals.
Animals too are living beings.
They get hurt just like us.
They too share their emotions among each other.
They have feelings.
They have families just like us.
Now they cannot speak to us directly—
Please stop, it's enough!!!

We kill them everyday, are we really humans?

God has made us intelligent so that we understand them. They cannot make us understand. The understanding has to come from us.

The dogs that are considered to be mad dogs are usually not mad, per se. They are treated as mad since they just bark at everyone and attack them suddenly. In fact, they are not mad; they are just fed up with the cruelty shown towards them by people. So they always remain alert and fearful, and try to keep the people away from them. This is a form of self-preservation, just like our instinct to defend ourselves from real and perceived potential harm. They are bound to do that. They have lost all their faith in humans. They now don't trust any people, whether good or bad. Humans have created so many threatening situations for them that they now look at us as their enemies.

If we can't do anything good for others then we also have no right to do anything bad to them.

We should be friendly with animals, as well as with other living species of this world. We all live on a single planet which we share, and each species

53

They have been waiting at our Gates with a hope that may
be one day we will understand their pain.

of creatures is influenced by the presence of other species. This is how
ecology is maintained. We should learn to live together with other species.
Only then, we will be able to know them better and we will also be able
to show them that we truly love them from our hearts.

*From today, let's make a promise to ourselves that
we won't harm them anymore.*

There are still so many species on this earth of which we know little or
nothing. Thus, this is the opportunity for all of us to know and understand
them in a better way—their life, their behaviour, their way of living—and
learn something from them that we humans lack.

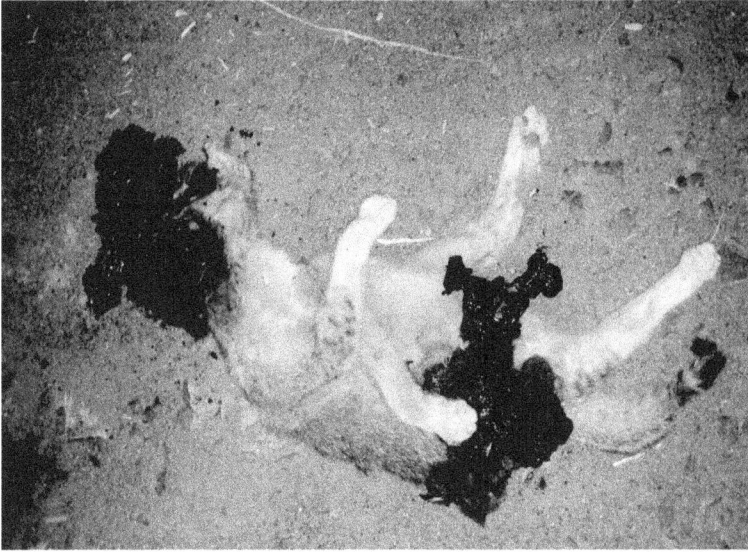

Think if it were you and nobody ever bothered.

Do you know?

Animals know better than us how to live better, happy, and genuine lives. It's true indeed! These are the species from which we need to learn many things. We need to understand them, their feelings, their needs...

They live in this world and all together we makeup this world. It can never be complete with the absence of any species from this planet. Together we maintain the ecosystem and contribute to it equally, and hence we need to understand the importance of each other and respect each other's presence. We can achieve nothing through conflict. Instead, we must step forward together, along with other species, towards a better, safer, and a brighter future.

We can conserve wildlife in many ways:

(i) **Provision of Animal Hospitals** – When we look for hospitals and doctors for ourselves, we can find several. But similarly, if we go looking for animal hospitals, we hardly find any. There are many reasons behind the lack of animal hospitals and veterinary doctors. This is because we hardly ever opt for such professions as we think it offers neither status nor is it lucrative. Today, if we ask ourselves how many of us are aiming to become a doctor, specialist, engineer, astronaut, accountant, entrepreneur, businessman, singer, dancer, actor, actress, film director/producer, animator, videographer, photographer, etc., there will be as many hands raised as available, but in the case of an animal doctor (veterinarian) or specialist, there will be very few who raise a hand, if at all.

Today, our choice of career is mostly determined by our love for money, but we usually don't admit that to others. Instead, people claim that they want to become engineers, doctors, entrepreneurs, etc., because they want to bring about a change or a development in that particular field. But there are very few people who aspire to really do something good and inspiring for society and mankind by pursuing such jobs. The truth is most people only want to earn money and dream about enjoying their lives like Gods in heaven.

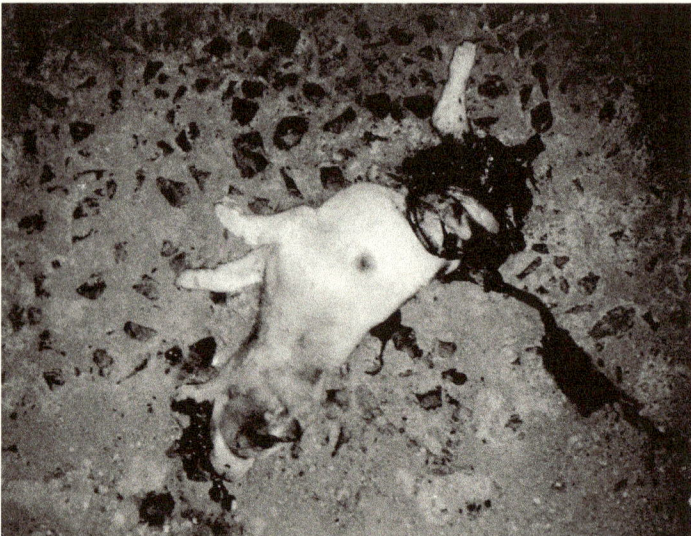

No Police, No Doctors, Where is the Justice?

One of the other reasons why people are reluctant to choose jobs in animal welfare is because they feel there is no prestige attached to serving animals. They don't see or understand importance of animals and wonder what will they gain if they serve the animals at the cost of their time and effort. In fact, they think there is something lowly about doing so. They forget that animals are crucial for maintaining balance in the ecology and the absence of animals will affect all human life and well-being. So, by saving animals we are in effect, saving our own lives.

Animals have been the best and the most trusted friends of mankind. They do not betray us like we do to ourselves. They are faithful to us for as long as they live on this earth. They do not give up on us, despite our thoughtlessness. They are innocent, important, precious, and incredible. They never come to us to ask anything for themselves, but we go to them for many things for ourselves. Sometimes it happens that we take many things from them, but we give them nothing in turn for what we get or take from them directly or indirectly. At least we should provide them food, shelter, love, and care, and respect them from our heart.

We need to open a large number of centers for the study, rescue, and rehabilitation of animals all over the world. We also need people with ability and compassion to opt for the profession of veterinarians irrespective of what they are paid; however, veterinarians do enjoy good pay scales with regular perks and upgradations like other professionals. There should be well-equipped ambulances in each hospital to transport the animals to hospitals in emergency cases, and police officers to provide protection to the animals that are in abusive situations. Provision of police for animals helps in informing the hospitals to send ambulances in emergency cases, and would also help in preventing the animals from being harmed by the people. We need dedicated support staffs who are totally devoted to wildlife with no hidden or self-profit motives. This is one way in which we can give our best to wildlife and save our environment, and, as all life on earth is interdependent, save our own lives as well.

(ii) Provision of Sanctuaries and Habitat – Although we have many sanctuaries for animals, we need more to accommodate the large number of animals who have lost their habitat. The sanctuaries must be well-equipped and, as far as possible, replicate the natural habitat of animals. There must be no industries or highways around/close to the sanctuaries so that the animals living in them can breathe in fresh air and take the advantage of a clean environment. Pollution can make animals prone to diseases. Having a pure and clean environment contributes to better health of the animals, and in turn, favours their breeding and healthy growth and ability to resist diseases that may harm the animals. The security guards in charge of sanctuaries, responsible for the animals

No food, no water, no shelter, where do they go?

living in them, must be honest and hardworking; they should not have any hidden motives or an eagerness to earn an extra income to fill their ever-empty pockets. They must be hard working and fully devoted to their work. Strict rules must be framed regarding the responsibilities of the guards. It must contain regulations which prevent guards from getting involved in any illegal activities regarding the animals in the reserves.

Illegal trafficking of animals and animal parts must be strictly dealt with by the Police and higher authorities. All sorts of systems with latest technologies must be implemented to track and record the number of animals living in the sanctuaries. The old ways of record keeping are error prone and easy to falsify which enables the culprits to pursue their illegal businesses with ease. Provision of security and fire alarms is also necessary in the sanctuaries for emergencies.

We must not forget that the real home of the animals is the forest, so the best thing we can do is to prevent forests from being cleared. We need to undertake extensive planting in order to compensate for the loss of forest cover due to our activities. This way, we can somewhat restore their lost habitat.

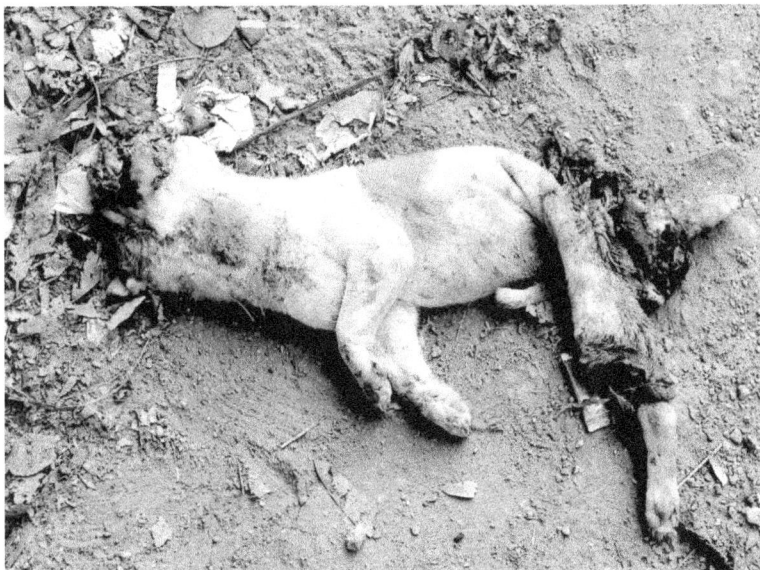

It shows why mother nature wouldn't forgive us.

(iii) Prevention of Cruelty to Animals – The next step is to setup more organizations across the world to deal with cases of cruelty towards animals—harmful treatment, overburdening of animals, and use of animals for entertainment and fun. Authorities should take strong actions against the torture and inhuman treatment of animals. Lastly, strict laws must be framed regarding the conduct of human beings towards animals and all people must obey and respect those rules. Severe punishments should be meted out to those violating any of these laws. More people need to be educated so that they can understand the importance of animals to our ecosystem and the importance of preserving them.

(iv) Making Animals our Friends – Yes, we need to make animals our friends, not for our own use but to help them co-exist with us peacefully. For instance, there are bound to be stray dogs and cats, outside our houses or shops. Let's provide them with food and fresh water. Let's not give them spoilt food or let them have sewage water. What is not fit for the human beings to eat or drink can be no way fit for animals. Play with them, they really like it—but do not play with their lives or harm them while playing. Do not even let others harm them in anyway. Make small shelters for them where they can take shelter during rain. Provide them your old clothes, so that they

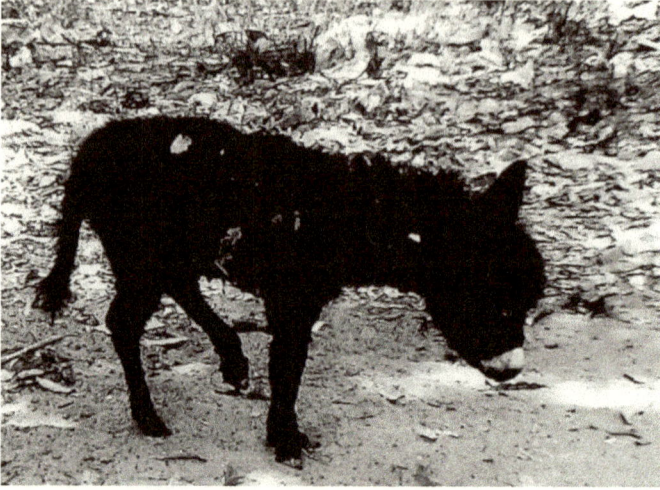

Don't their babies deserve love, but we make
them lame—is that our love?

do not shiver in the cold. They may not get to have cool air from air conditioners during hot summer, but I believe they absolutely deserve to be sheltered from the burning sun. They have always been faithful to us, and now I think it's our turn to show that we can do better in fulfilling our obligations to them. Remember, a beggar can pretend to be hungry so that you may donate him some money, but an animal will never pretend that it is hungry or needs help because it doesn't know what "truth", "lie", and "betrayal" are. So when an animals seems hungry, take it seriously.

(v) **Control your Pleasures and Self-Defense Techniques** – Don't trap butterflies, dragonflies, and moths for pleasure. Don't unnecessarily kill snakes claiming self-defense. They don't harm us unless we confront them directly or indirectly. There are many other species of animals which we harm or kill to save ourselves or our property. But that is not the right way to tackle them. They can be caught in cages, and then released in the forest, or at some place where they will be safe from us as well as we will be safe from them. They wander among us, mostly in search of food and shelter as we have slowly occupied their lands and hunting grounds till they have nowhere else to go.

(vi) **Invite them on Occasions and Ceremonies** – Usually, they don't require an invitation, they appear without any cue from us. The smell of delicious food automatically attracts them. Whether it is a wedding ceremony or a birthday party, if you ever see any animal—be it dog, cat, cow, or goat—sitting or standing outside, waiting for food, just pick up a plate or two with all the food items that they would really love to eat and go and serve them as if they were your guests too. They feel very hungry when they pick up the smell of food items being cooked. In fact, we all feel hungry when that happens, but unfortunately animals cannot come to us directly and say that they are hungry. I have seen them many times waiting outside such places but nobody even bothers to look at them. Believe me, we lose nothing when we serve four or five plates of food to these hungry animals instead of people. And you will feel quite blessed when you see them eating.

(vii) **Support Wildlife Organizations** – Another way to conserve wildlife is to support (volunteer) and donate to organizations that are associated with the conservation of wildlife and environment which are really successful in what they do and try to achieve. We need to support the organizations which work to preserve this world and in which we can believe. Till today, these organizations have saved millions and billions of animals from death and helped preserve endangered species from becoming extinct. They have also helped in protecting their habitat and ensured a better future for wildlife over the course of time. These organizations and their people are very hard working and completely dedicated to wildlife. All this would not have been possible without the support and involvement of the common people like us who care about the wildlife and understand its importance. The more we donate, the better they are able to serve the animals. As everyone knows, animals do not earn money like people. We have made that compulsory for human beings to live, but we did not anticipate that because of our system the animals would end up suffering the most. Animals have the same right to this planet's resources as we have, but we have simply dominated them because we have grown quite powerful and possessive, becoming a threat to the survival of all other living species on this planet.

viii) **Forge a new system for Animal Welfare** – Animals cannot earn money like us that they can use to live a proper life in a world we have created on our own, where everything depends on money, even life. They cannot benefit anything from our current economic system— made only for humans. Instead, the other species of this planet have been suffering because of our system, which is mostly advantageous to our life and not theirs. Hence, we need to forge a new system for animals, where all the animals, as well as other species, shall have food, water, and shelter at no cost. We must take into account that they have the right to use the available resources on this planet as well, but we have simply dominated them and made our own system that is only beneficial to us, leaving the rest of the species of this world to suffer among us and perish. It shows how careless and selfish we have always been. We've cared for none but ourselves. We may not persist with the declining number of animals from this planet.

Therefore, it is essential for us and our government to foresee our ruined future due to the absence of other species from this planet. And hence, create such a system that is helpful and beneficial to *all* the living beings of this world and not just humans. We all live together and so we should take care of each other, instead of caring only for ourselves. Not only should they get food, water, and shelter free of cost, but also all medical services required when they are sick or are injured, completely free of cost. Why should they pay any money to us? Did we ever consider them as a part of our life before we created our great economic system? But they have always considered us as their friends—someone they can trust. Were we so blind to fulfill our needs for a great comfortable life that we couldn't see that the other species were equally important for humans to survive on this planet? How did we simply leave them to suffer and die with no hope from mankind? When in fact, it has always been our responsibility to look after these less fortunate helpless species who are not blessed with intelligence like us. Our knowledge is only useful and a boon when it is beneficial to all life on this planet and not just us. We must use our knowledge to make everybody's life better, including this planet. Only then can we expect a better life and future for the generations ahead, or else they will have to suffer and pay for our mistakes.

Think of a child with a gun and a giant lion. If there is a fight between the two, who do you think will win and how long will the battle go on? It will take only a second or two for the child to point the gun at the lion's head and pull the trigger—the lion will be dead in no time. That's how powerful humans are. What makes us so powerful sits inside our skull—the brain. Yes, it is human intelligence that makes us so powerful and helps us dominate other species. At the same time, it is this intelligence which is a big threat to us. Now, how will animals be given their rights on this planet? Who will give them justice? When will this dominance end? These are indeed big questions, and the answers lie within us. We are humans above all, and we know well what is good and what is bad in what we do. Now it's up to us whether we allow the good in us to dominate our lives and make it successful, or let the evil in us destroy our lives as well as the lives of others and lay the whole planet to waste.

While there are people who let the bad in them dominate over the good, who harm all the species on this planet, and care for none, going beyond any limit to possess what they want at any cost, be it the lives of the innocent, there are also people who are good and who actually help everyone, and understand the pain, grief and importance of each and every living species on this planet. In fact, it will be the good humans who will defend all other species of this planet, either by transforming the bad ones into good or by going into battle for what is good, and neutralizing the efforts of the wrongdoers to ensure that the planet does not suffer anymore in the wrong hands. Only time will tell who wins this battle, and that will decide the future of this planet and all its living inhabitants.

Education and Jobs: The Loss of Significance

For what do we pursue education? For most of us, we want to get a good job so that we can earn money. For some, this indicates that they hardly have any larger aim in life. They just want to be driven by others, but wherever they're taken doesn't matter. All they need is the money so that they may stay alive, and yes, enjoy life of course! Well, this is one of the major reasons why we still act like uneducated people. Many people never understand the full value of an education. Education was never meant to get us a good job so that we can simply start earning money. It was meant to give us the knowledge required to be good and responsible human beings. It was meant to reveal our dreams and make them happen for real. Money will never give you the power to decide between what is wrong and what is right; it is education that enhances your decision-making power. Life is so meaningless when earning money becomes your only aim. The aim of life should be to endeavour, to contribute to the history of mankind, and deliver something valuable to humanity. We simply waste our life when we spend it pursuing none other than what we created ourselves. If you are still dreaming of having a big house with two Mercedes parked out front, then money has already corrupted your potential. Think of your childhood days when you never knew what money was, when you spent your days doing what you liked to do the most or what has always influenced you the most—that is what you should have grown up to be. And believe me, if you had kept that precious feeling alive, you could have worked for that dream, and been what you most wanted to be, instead of living up to the expectations of society.

Dreams are not so easy to achieve as earning money is. But money should always be your second choice with your dreams being the first, in all that you do, whether it is your education or your job. I still remember when I grew up and my family gave "getting a good job so that I can earn good money" as the primary reason to pursue higher education. It felt so absurd and meaningless, and since then I decided that I would rather prefer dying to a life spent chasing money. Is this for what we are really born? Is this for what we live? Is this the true destiny of human beings? Are we so unintelligent that we don't even know where we should be heading? I don't want to run after something that everybody can have!

I want to run after something that humans haven't seen before and that is what makes my life more meaningful, fulfilling, and complete. I want to live and work so that I can give back something to humanity, to this planet, and become an inspiration for the coming generation, so that they know what is more important in life.

Education is not for getting a good job; it is for innovation, knowledge, and the power to make the right decisions at the right time.

"You know, nothing is more important than education, because nowhere are our stakes higher; our future depends on the quality of education of our children today."

– Arnold Schwarzenegger

Always study what you really want to learn about or what really excites you. Educate yourself so that you can be a good human being and a responsible citizen of planet earth. Educate yourself so that you will know how to solve problems in your life safely and perfectly, develop your skills, and strengthen your decision-making power so that you will always know what is right for you, and others, or this planet.

Don't make education a need, make it a purpose. When you are in school or college, understand what you are struggling for—what the purpose of your life is. Do not waste your life or your time in anything that doesn't teach you something good or something valuable which can later help you be what you always wanted to be. Time is running out and nobody knows what happens next. So make your way and live your dreams. Be always purposeful. Make your life meaningful and don't keep it aimless, otherwise you will be lost. And when you are lost, money, as well as the wrong people, start driving you in the direction they want you to go for their own benefit and you lose all your control, which can lead to the destruction of your life by resulting in you becoming a thief, a murderer, or anything that is quite harmful to humanity or this planet.

Don't let others drive you; your life is not useless. It is yours and you should live for your dreams, not just to run after material things or simply to be used by people. Know who you are, the future lies within you. And you lead the future of this planet. Be the best that you can be and give to the generations ahead. This makes your life complete. Every life on this earth has a purpose and we must attain it before we die. ***Know the purpose of your life*** and start working on it until you reach your destination; that will make your life successful.

> *"For me life is continuously being hungry. The meaning of life is not simply to exist, to survive, but to move ahead, to go up, to achieve, to conquer."*
>
> *– Arnold Schwarzenegger*

When people reach or acquire higher positions in life, most often they forget what they were, from where they came, how they used to be. All that then matters to them is their name, fame, pride, and possessions. And yet, that is what proves to be the reason for their loss of everything—sometimes even life. Love and respect is quite valuable, it takes a lot of good deeds to earn, but lasts much longer than a name, fame, and possessions. It is what binds our souls with trust and strength. One may lose everything in life but not the love and respect he has earned, even after his death.

*To all the precious children of Mother Earth, make a promise that you will **never use your knowledge to cause pain or problems for your mother**. Instead, use your knowledge to always protect her. She wishes to enjoy our progress with us, together, but never let your progress bring her pain and misery. She cannot speak, and cannot tell you she is in pain. As a child, it is our duty to form a protective blanket, so that no one can harm her anymore. When we were small, she was the ground where we stood for the first time and still do so now. It's our turn to take her responsibilities on our shoulders now that she is in need. After all, she lives in us and we live in her. We are one and all forever.*

Election of Leaders (Ministers and Presidents)

Always choose as your leader one who is responsible and is in favour of what is right. Do not support anyone who fulfills his own motives by resting his feet on your shoulders. His motive should have good intent and stand for what is right for humanity, as well as for animals and this planet. Yes, sometimes he might be human-friendly but not eco-friendly, so keep it in mind if he is not in favour of animals and the environment then he is no way in favour of you, your family, or your nation. He is simply misdirecting people for his own purpose. Your leader should be your voice and not his own. Always see that he is not arrogant, over confident, promising more luxuries than focusing on needs, harming others in the name of defending the nation or its people. Surely you can tell that such people are unfit to be your leader. One who doesn't value the importance of life or finds pleasure in harming others can never stand for humanity, this planet, or any of its life forms. Remember, we are not alone. We need to think about what is best for this entire planet and all life forms on it, because we all live together and we are the ones blessed with intelligence on this earth. That is how we truly fulfill our responsibilities as human beings.

> *"To restore the trust of the people, we must reform the way the government operates."*
>
> *– Arnold Schwarzenegger*

> *"When the people become involved in their government, government becomes more accountable, and our society is stronger, more compassionate, and better prepared for the challenges of the future."*
>
> *– Arnold Schwarzenegger*

There must be a new rule formulated and enforced for all the Ministers and Presidents of the world, in which, if a leader who has been elected, does not function properly or up to the expectations of the general people, then the people should have an option for negative voting. And when this negative vote goes above 50% of the votes that had been received during election, then the leader will have to surrender his position and a new election will be held to choose another capable leader. There should be no such thing as once they have been elected, they can do anything they like for a term of five years without any repercussion. Such a five-year term might become an enjoyment for the elected leader and create too much suffering for the people. Winning an election does not give the leader license to play with the lives of common people or enjoy great luxurious living, forgetting all their responsibilities and promises which they make to the people before the election. Those days are gone when the public could be led in the direction the politicians wanted, because now they are facing an educated society where most people know what is right or wrong for their lives and the nation.

So, he who does not work for the welfare of the people, his nation, or this planet, should have to surrender his powers of leadership to someone who is responsible, and capable of taking charge. Those powers are not for him to rule this world and its people, but to solve their problems, help them progress, and manage the nation. Those powers come from the common people, if they can give it, they should have the right to withdraw it.

Once this law is enforced, from then on, no leader will make anymore fake promises to the people, for he will know that his powers can be withdrawn anytime. It is then he will become careful, responsible, and committed to his duties, bring peace, harmony, and uplift a nation and its people, and hence serve as an example to this world. A leader should be the strength of the people, not the source of their suffering.

One right decision can lead us to destinies; whereas, one wrong decision can lead us to chaos. Hence, decide wisely before choosing your leader.

We are the World

Have you ever imagined how this world would be, how our lives would be, how our environment would be, if all humans—all the people of this world, and all the children become completely and strongly united.

We are one and the same.

We are all human beings—a single species.

We are the World.

We humans need to have complete unity among ourselves. Then people will take care of each other, respect each other, be friendly with each other, share resources among each other, and there will be no existence of jealousy, only love, love, and love everywhere, all over the world.

Patriotism has been a major factor which stands in the way of world unity because people interpret it in very different ways that are often isolating. It was never meant to create differences among people or countries; still, they do not understand that love for one's country doesn't mean hate for the rest, but equally respecting other countries too. When a country is formed, people are separated from people around the whole world and a name is assigned to each group of people living on a particular piece of land, which denotes the boundaries of the country. Not only people are separated among themselves but the whole earth is divided into pieces. When we say: this is my country, that is his country, and the other is their country (fighting or arguing among ourselves), then the unity among the people of this whole world is compromised. This is indeed one of the major reasons why wars take place between countries. We feel a sense of complete unity when we say that we live on earth and we are the world or together we form the world. Hence, all the countries of this world are like brothers and sisters. And if you are really a patriot then you should know well that being patriotic means being responsible for the reputation of your country, so when you disrespect any other country, you simply disrespect your own country by proving yourself such a backward thinking citizen of your country. ***Learn to respect and love all the people of this world before expecting the same from the people for yourself.***

So what are you?

Are you Indian, American, African, Japanese, Russian, Chinese, French or Australian?

Whatever you might be, you cannot escape from the truth that we all live in a single home which is Earth. And a home is that heavenly place where people live with love and care. And we, the people of this world, are just like members of a family living in a single home. We should care for each other, share our innermost thoughts, joy, grief, and the available resources among ourselves. We should have love in our hearts for each other. If you believe in complete unity then you should say – I am a human being, a citizen of this world, and I live on this incredible blue-green earth, happily with my family, safe and secure.

Thus, the need for the formation of a country should be only for better maintenance of that particular piece of land and lives of the people living there. Countries should not be used to create differences among people. We should not even fight for lands because we all have equal rights to Mother Earth, rather, if there is a scarcity or a need, we must share it and that would be the best choice for all of us. We are all human beings and we can understand better each other's problems, difficulties and needs, hence we can take better decisions on behalf of us all.

The great leaders of the world or of different countries had to struggle hard for independence for all of us. Why?

It's because when a few groups of people across the world gained power with the help of their knowledge, they thought of ruling over the rest. They grew selfish and wanted to enjoy all the luxuries of life by torturing those people who were comparatively not so intelligent and hence less powerful. Due to their selfish character, they lost humanity and blindly continued pandering to their selfish deeds. If they had understood that we are all human beings, we are the same, a part of one family, a single species living in a single home—earth, then they would have behaved differently. They would have shared their knowledge with those less fortunate and improved their lives. Thus, great leaders across the world would not have had to struggle for independence and lose their precious lives. There would have been no loss of life and property. Rather, the world would have progressed much better. A better and safe world would have been formed.

"Knowledge will give you power, but character respect."

– *Bruce Lee*

We know very well that nobody in this world likes wars. Every one of us needs to have a safe and peaceful life. In spite of this, just because of the Presidents of different countries and their Defense Departments, wars come into existence. And in this, only the satisfaction of few hundred people is involved while the rest of the people of this world are not allowed to voice their suggestions or register their disapproval. Thus, if we take notice of why wars actually take place, then we find that it is often because of the people who are elected by the common people of this world to look after their problems, progress, and take the right decisions. But these elected people often try to overtake each other in terms of power, and destroy so many lives in the name of "self-defense", thereby identifying each other as threats. Due to this kind of wrong mindedness, many people around the whole world lose their precious lives. There occurs severe loss of life and property.

What is the gain?

Only the people who are elected into office by the common people gain power, money, land, all luxuries, etc. But what about the common people on whose behalf they are supposed to govern? They lose their most precious thing—life. They lose their shelter and property. Children lose their parents. Parents lose their children. The situation becomes so bad that though their bodies keep living, their souls become dead.

Not only this, have you ever considered how much loss of our environment our planet suffers every time due to wars? Destruction of our environment in these cases is intense and there is severe toll on the animal population too. Why do animals and the environment always have to be the victim of our mistakes? They don't even understand why they are condemned to die painful deaths, either with gunshots or explosions. How can humans rain destruction upon them when the fight is not of their making?

Our leaders make the decision to go to war but the ones who suffer from the fallout are the common people, innocent animals, and the helpless environment. Our leaders need to understand that they cannot put the lives of common people at risk for whatever decisions they take.

They are elected for the welfare of the common people, to represent their countries and for this world. Instead of handling tense situations wisely, if they lead us into war then they have failed as leaders and betrayed our trust. ***Killing innocent people and animals is neither self-defense nor leadership.*** It is simply a lack of the right kind of education and abuse of power. ***Decisions must be always in favour of humanity and mankind, peace without any destruction, and solving of problems through mutual understanding, support and collaboration.*** Our leaders do not have the right to take decisions on our behalf which involve risking our lives or lives of people in other countries.

We pay taxes, they build weapons in the name of self-defense, and later they use those weapons to kill the common people of this world. So next time, you should check whether your taxable money is actually used for the welfare of the common people, or for indiscriminate warfare. Otherwise you become partly responsible for the deaths of innocent children, their parents, brothers and sisters, and animals from around the world, it doesn't matter which country they are from, what matters is that you are involved in the loss of humanity and mankind. What if the general public in other countries invest money in building weapons which their leaders decide to use to kill your children or entire family? Would you like to be at the receiving end of this injustice? Obviously not. Then how can you do the same? Why are you putting funds into making weapons that lead to lives ending and the death of humanity!? If the weapons are to combat invading aliens from space then it will perhaps prove beneficial as we will be using them to protect our planet. But here, we mostly use them to kill people—be they soldiers or civilians.

Henceforth, whenever the danger of war arises, all people must withdraw their support for their lost-minded leaders and march against their harmful decisions. We know very well that there are no winners in a war and the one who is going to be the victim is us. Therefore, we must withdraw our support before our hands are red with the blood of innocents. I don't understand why our leaders think that killing each other's people can resolve long-standing issues or bring peace and harmony to the world. Why are they always so arrogant and aggressive? Why don't they understand that we are all humans with needs and problems, but killing each other is not the solution. ***When will we learn to collaborate with each other, cooperate with each other, understand each other's problems, and solve them together as one family?*** When will we learn that we are one family? Why do we always forget our own saying—United we stand, divided we fall? All that matters is we are all humans and we all belong to one family and a single home which is our earth.

Animals fight among themselves in competition for food. What happens? The one who wins, survives, and the other dies of hunger. But if they share the food, both can survive. Why does this happen?

This is only because they don't have reasoning and decision-making abilities. Now if we humans do the same thing (fight) among ourselves for resources, then, what is the difference between us and the animals? In spite of having reasoning and decision-making abilities, we act like animals. So, we must always try to share the resources—that will be the best choice for all humanity. Moreover, caring and sharing makes our relationship stronger. It enhances the bonds between us. A safe and peaceful life is only possible when we change our way of thinking, improve it, be optimistic, and remove all the differences and inequalities existing among us. We should learn from our past so that mistakes committed in the past may not be repeated by us once again in the future. And since our present decides the nature of the coming future, we should first pay attention to our present.

When we make a decision to follow a particular religion, we are free to do so as per our choice. But we have no right to force our religion on other people who are often already following other religious denominations. As it has been written in most of the religious books like the Bible, the Bhagavad Gita, and the Quran, etc., I believe that there is one God but our modes of worshipping him are varied. Therefore, if we follow one way, and some other people follow a different way, then it doesn't matter at all, because the motive behind all the different ways is one and the same i.e., to connect to God. Religion consists of those ways which our forefathers decided to follow in order to connect to God—which is a single aim that all the religions have. We should recognize this and not go to war over our religious differences.

We should not create something which later becomes a threat to the lives of people, our own lives, and the survival of the planet. I am talking about weapons like guns, T.N.T. bombs, atomic and hydrogen bombs, etc. and now we are marching towards the most devastating of all—the anti-matter bomb. We should understand that these weapons of mass destruction provide us enormous power, and when we gain power, we generally become blind and lose our power to make right or safe decisions, and then we start to act blindly where we mostly tend to misuse our powers, knowingly or unknowingly.

Do you know?

Man is not by himself innately dangerous or a threat to his own existence, but it is their love for conflict which makes humans dangerous and a threat to the race. We say that we have invented all these equipment/weapons for our security or for the security of countries from one another. What kind of convoluted attempt is this to establish peace? Rather, it leads to the destruction of peace. If the weapons had never been created then the terrorists could never have used them to cause any destruction to mankind. Weapons are not a curse to us, but we have let them become a curse by letting them fall into the wrong hands. *With weapons falling into the wrong hands, we are preparing to end our own lives.* If we become united then there will be no need for national security to protect countries from one another; instead, the security against the terrorism will become stronger since all our efforts will be concentrated on a single agenda.

We should not use weapons to make decisions but we should use our heart. We should not speak in terms of power but we should speak in words of love.

We always feel that what we have is not enough or sufficient for us to live our life. We can't escape it because this is one of the characteristics that we, as human beings, possess. We always wish to have luxury goods like refrigerators, air conditioners, art-works, gold and diamond ornaments, mobile phones, cars, high-quality furniture, clothes, boots, cosmetics, etc. Meanwhile, if we take a look at the poor, sometimes they don't even have a roof to take shelter under; they don't have proper clothes to cover their bodies, and they cannot even afford enough food to survive. Thus, between all our desires, if we sacrifice one or two of them, then our quality of life will hardly be affected. Instead, it can fulfill the needs of many poor people.

"Help others and give something back. I guarantee you will discover that while public service improves the lives and the world around you, its greatest reward is the enrichment and new meaning it will bring your own life."

– Arnold Schwarzenegger

When we get more, we expect more. In such cases we should control our desires and put a limit on our indulgence. We should be satisfied with what we have and what God has given us. We should not let desire make us greedy. If we sacrifice some of our desires then the needs of our brothers and sisters can be fulfilled. Moreover, if we won't help each other in times of need then who else is going to help? Many think that only God can help—but God helps those who help themselves.

We should share our love and resources among ourselves.

We should support each other in times of pleasure and grief.

We should share our knowledge and achievements among ourselves.

We can only make good progress if we are united and work together.

Hard work never goes wasted; it always gives you something valuable in turn. Moreover, combined effort produces better results than individual effort. There are many examples for this and one such is NASA (National Aeronautics Space Administration), where people from all over the world work together and the results of that are clearly before us. NASA has progressed a lot and has achieved several goals since its establishment. It has improved normal lives, not only in one or two countries but around the whole world. And today, it has become one of the fastest and most progressive research organizations in the world. This shows us that collaborating globally can really bring better changes to human life within a short period of time.

If we won't help each other and forge a world of love, care, and sharing as a family then we can never progress completely in our lives. We can never feel that our life is purposeful or fulfilling.

So let us come together and lend a helping hand to the needy, eradicate the differences existing among us and in our minds, and put an end to dominance. Let's make this earth an incredibly cleaner, safer, and better place—a heaven for coming generations.

"I am the most helpful and open up doors for everyone and I like to share."

– Arnold Schwarzenegger

We will not go separate ways.

We will go one way united.

Wars and conflicts are not the solutions to peace but cooperating with each other, discussing the problems of each other, and negotiating safe solutions is the right and safe way to peace. This way we can hope for a better future for our children and coming generations.

All we need to survive on this blue-green planet is to cooperate with each other and develop an attitude of caring and sharing among ourselves while we try to eradicate greed and jealousy from our minds, and inspire future generations to embrace these sterling traits, which are going to finally make this earth a beautiful and sweet home for one and all forever.

Stopping the Evil in You

So, what makes us a bad person and when? Well, the very first time we start to feel pleasant, even though we know we did something wrong, is probably a sign that we are crossing over to the wrong side. This is especially evident when other people start to call us bad. Still, how would we know what is considered wrong? Well, this is the reason why we get an education. Education gives us the required knowledge to help decide what is good and what is bad.

If you want to be a really good person then you will do good at all costs. However, it is not so easy when your environment is filled with destructive things and negative people. Some persist in doing good, while others succumb to temptation. Whenever you see a bad thing, try not to let that stay in your mind. It is human nature that we perceive the bad more easily than the good. So *the best way is to keep ourselves away from the bad as far as possible*. Sometimes, we tend to have a bad circle of friends who influence us to be like them. It is better to be friendless than keeping a bad company. Instead, make books your friends, make animals your friends, make your brothers, sisters, and parents your friends, as well as being your own best friend.

Another way is *not to dwell on the bad*. Try to listen to your good side even when everything else around you is bad, and try to persuade the good inside you to dominate over your evil side. How much you are able to control yourself in doing that determines whether you will be a good person or a bad. If negative thoughts enter our minds, it is because we let them in. Whereas, sometimes we are not able to stop it because something makes us feel immensely pleasant in the beginning, but then it starts to ruin our life and we don't even realize because we usually ignore it for so long that everything ends up spiraling completely out of control.

It is better to stop yourself the very first time when you start to fall into a cycle of bad decision, because the deeper you get into it, the more difficult it becomes for you to get out of it.

Look, when I was in school, at first, I had no friends because I was absolutely good. Then after a few days, I got one friend, then two, three and so on. I realized that they were also good. After a few years, a boy came into our class who was really disruptive. As days went on, one by one all my friends started resorting to bad conduct due to his influence. Soon, almost every one of them was affected, except for one or two who somehow stayed away from his influence, like I did. I started losing friends, not exactly by breaking up friendships, but by slowly distancing myself. The bad boy had more friends than anyone else. He was like a disease that infected all my friends. I started going to the library when everyone went to play. I did feel lonely, but at the same time, books began grabbing my interest. I read as many science books as possible and I fell in love with science.

Within 3 years, there were no more science, physics, chemistry, biology, zoology books or encyclopedias left in the library that I hadn't read! I even knew where each word was on which page of which book and in which stack of books it could be found. After that, I started considering teachers my friends. This gave me much more confidence. I knew teachers would never ruin my life. Indeed, they would scold me, punish me, but I knew it was all for my good. I needed no friends then; however, I did have one or two who liked me and kept me company most of the time. They too spurned bad influences.

As time went by, I was able to win the trust of the teachers, and then one day I made a written complaint to one of my teachers who was very strict. Many teachers went through that written complaint, after which, it was submitted to the principal who was even stricter. The next day, the boy was suspended from the school right before the exams. Everyone realized that that's what happens when you are a bad person and how it ruins one's life if one doesn't get into the right path at the right time. Finally, I got back all my friends; however, some of them were quite ruined, but tried to improve before their entire life got destroyed. I won! I gained a great amount of knowledge from my book friends, love from the teachers, and ultimately, I had more friends than anyone else. I had the power of good within myself with which I was able to turn most of my friends back to the right path. I was even popular with everybody's family. Obviously, parents want you to make good friends in life rather than bad ones.

From the above scenario, you will realize that going down the wrong path is quite easy; it even seems like good fun in the beginning! But as time goes on, your great future starts turning dark, and ultimately is destroyed. Such a life span is usually short. While it is a little hard sometimes to be a good person—you may face many criticisms, jokes, bullying, etc., but your life is stronger and longer. You get everything you want, just a little later, and not right in the beginning. You need to work hard, be strong, and stay on the straight path to get results, but it is worth it. You will benefit from it your whole life.

In order to be a good person, just **keep yourself connected to God, parents, teachers, good books, good movies, and good friends**. The more you keep yourself away from bad influences, the safer you will be. Sometimes, you just need to confront wrongdoers, be strong, and don't let them contaminate your mind, heart, or soul. Strengthen the good in you and allow it to flourish in your life so that the bad in you never gets the chance to rise and ruin your life.

The battle between good and evil begins within yourself; the side that wins is what you choose it to be, and that is what decides the destiny of your life.

Final Words

So, let's say you have forgotten everything you've read in this book. Don't panic! Actually, some information has percolated into your mind; it is only a matter of time when you recall it at will. Still, I know how difficult it is to retain each and everything in your memory. So, to make it easy, I have prepared a small list of primary and very specific steps in short points that you can always put into use:

"If it's hard to remember, it'll be difficult to forget."

– Arnold Schwarzenegger

- Gain knowledge on what causes pollution, over-exploitation of natural resources, felling of trees, and killing of animals, and try to prevent them as soon as, and as much as possible.

- Do not waste. Do not pollute. Do not misuse or overuse. Save electricity and all forms of energy, water, coal, oil, trees, and animals. This will help save the planet from most forthcoming dangers.

- Plant trees and spread the awareness and knowledge to help educate people. Do anything (legally) to protect trees and increase their population.

- Raise your voice against the wrong, withdraw your support for who do wrong or stand for it, while supporting the people and organizations that stand for good.

- Stop using anything that harms the environment directly or indirectly.

- Encourage paying carbon tax. Every company and shop must make donations for the environment every month. Even small contributions can make big things happen. Donate to your favourite and trusted organizations that you know really work. You can always get a report on how your money is being utilized.

- Do not weigh the value of everything in terms of money. There are many things that can never be compensated for, no matter how much money we put in.

- Be caring, loving, and helpful to all the animals, trees, and humans as a part of your family. This world is your family after all, with earth being our single and beautiful home.

Overall, be a good, caring, and a responsible human being.

Rescuing our 'mom' is not just rescuing Mother Earth from global warming and climate change, but all issues that put her life at risk and threaten the existence of all living organisms of this ever-beautiful planet. We need to understand that nothing is going to become right on this earth unless we make an effort to align our mind and soul with the environment, working towards what is right for this planet and our lives. It is only then that we will embody the true purpose for being human, and our planet will not have to suffer anymore. The world we create lies in our hands. This is going to be the inspiring history of humans on mother earth. *The history that inspires the future.*

The world is transforming. You would like to be a part of it, wouldn't you? Behave in such a way that tomorrow you will feel proud that you too have contributed to this change. And of course, it will not be possible without you.

Nature is incredibly beautiful, preserve it.

This whole time, you have been reading information on conserving the future, saving the future, making the future better, safe, brighter, and all that, but what exactly is that future? The answer is right there in a line from a popular movie – Terminator: "*There is no fate but what we make*". Yes, the future never comes pre-made to us; it is what we make it today. Tomorrow, your today becomes your past while tomorrow becomes your present that you will be creating. So consider always making your present better and better as the days go by, and your future will obviously be better. Creating hell in the present, knowing that somebody has foretold that your future is bright, is a certain way to ruin your whole life and your *readymade* future will never happen the way you are expecting it. What you do today, and how you do it, will determine where will you be tomorrow. Hence, make today the best you can. Don't ruin your today because today is what you had been waiting for yesterday.

Today is the tomorrow that you had been waiting for yesterday.

Always nurture happiness within yourself that will make you feel cherished and live longer, rather than harbouring greed, jealousy, and rudeness within you. That will only create problems for you as well as others, making your life more difficult and shorter in time.

Do something that lets you be happy for longer, rather than running after something that brings you immense joy for a short time and later turns into pain and sorrow.

Don't do anything which may later make your life a burden to yourself and others.

By the time you close this book, I wish to see a changed person. You are going to be the real hero who saves the whole planet from all the dangers that it could face until your last breath. You are going to make your present the best, and hence we can look forward to a better tomorrow.

The world waits for you to act. And your 'mom' awaits your valuable response.

When you rescue your 'mom', you rescue yourself.

A right step taken at the right time can keep us away from facing serious problems.

Your awakening stops the holocaust.

List of Nonprofit Organizations

Below is a list of almost 60+ Nonprofit Organizations which work to protect and conserve the environment, wildlife, natural resources, oceans and of course, humans. You can support the organizations that you find best, in a number of ways. To explore the ways, be sure to visit their websites and select "Get Involved", "Adopt", "Take Action", "Become a Member or Guardian", "Fundraising", "Sponsor" or "Donate" or anything that shows how you can support them. You can help them by promoting their work on social media, etc., by signing petitions, taking pledges, taking action, fundraising, donating, volunteering, etc. Be a part of any organization or a group of organizations and see how pleasant you feel when you realize that you helped them achieve something good and significant that either saved someone's life or helped someone get a plate of food or shelter to live in, or made change possible. When you do good, you start feeling happy from deep within your heart and it appears all on your face, and we all see it.

There are in fact a lot more organizations working quite hard to save our planet and its inhabitants from the problems and dangers that beset it, but I couldn't list them all here as I need to keep this book short and easy on pocket. However, you can always find most of the organizations on the internet and you can support them as you wish. All you need is—just take action. They do all the work making huge projects possible every year, which we otherwise could never have achieved alone. So, all they need is our generous support in achieving their goals, which are in fact to make this planet and our life better as well as safe.

This list is also available on the book's website – "www.rescueyourmom.org/organizations" along with relevant information where you can find direct links to these organizations at the comfort of your fingertips.

1) National Geographic Society

www.nationalgeographic.org

The National Geographic Society is a nonprofit scientific and educational organization dedicated to exploring our planet, protecting wildlife and habitats, and helping assure that school leavers are geographically literate. It was founded in 1888 "to increase and diffuse geographic knowledge". The Society believes in the power of science, exploration and storytelling to change the world. Its purpose is to inspire, illuminate and teach. National Geographic is governed by a board of trustees, whose 21 members include distinguished educators, business executives, former government officials and conservationists.

For almost 130 years, they have funded groundbreaking scientists and explorers and shared their findings with the world. They sponsored Hiram Bingham as he brought back stories of Machu Picchu, documented Robert Ballard's quest to find the Titanic, and supported Jane Goodall's study of chimpanzees. Their explorers continue to push the boundaries of knowledge. To date, they've given out more than 12,000 grants to scientists and conservationists whose work is making a real difference in the world.

They support critical projects like the Big Cats Initiative, which is working to stop the decline in populations of big cats in the wild; and the Pristine Seas project, which has helped protect 3 million square kilometers of the ocean's last wild places. They rely on the support of generous donors to fund their work in research, education, and conservation around the world.

2) World Wide Fund for Nature (World Wildlife Fund)

www.worldwildlife.org

The World Wide Fund for Nature (WWF) is an international non-governmental organization founded in 1961, working in the field of the wilderness preservation, and the reduction of humanity's footprint on the environment. It was formerly named the World Wildlife Fund, which remains its official name in Canada and the United States.

It is the world's largest conservation organization with over 5 million supporters worldwide, working in more than 100 countries, supporting around 1,300 conservation and environmental projects. WWF is a foundation, with 55% of funding from individuals and bequests, 19% from government sources (such as the World Bank, DFID, USAID) and 8% from corporations in 2014.

The group's mission is "to stop the degradation of the planet's natural environment and to build a future in which humans live in harmony with nature." Currently, much of its work focuses on the conservation of three biomes that contain most of the world's biodiversity: oceans and coasts, forests, and freshwater ecosystems. Among other issues, it is also concerned with endangered species, sustainable production of commodities and climate change.

3) Rainforest Action Network (RAN)

www.ran.org

Rainforest Action Network campaigns for the forests, their inhabitants and the natural systems that sustain life by transforming the global marketplace through education, grassroots organizing and non-violent direct action.

It is an environmental organization based in San Francisco, California, United States. The organization was founded by Randy "Hurricane" Hayes and Mike Roselle in 1985, and first gained national prominence with a grassroots organizing campaign that, in 1987, succeeded in convincing Burger King to cancel $35 million worth of destructive Central American rainforest beef contracts. Protecting forests and challenging corporate power has remained a key focus of RAN's campaigns since, and has led RAN into campaigns that have led to transformative policy changes across home building, wood purchasing and supplying, automobile, fashion, paper and banking industries.

4) People for the Ethical Treatment of Animals (PETA)

www.peta.org

"People for the Ethical Treatment of Animals (PETA)" is an American animal rights organization based in Norfolk, Virginia, and led by Ingrid Newkirk, its international president. A nonprofit corporation with 300 employees, it claims that it has 3 million members and supporters (5 million in total) and is the largest animal rights group in the world. Its slogan is "animals are not ours to eat, wear, experiment on, use for entertainment, or abuse in any other way."

Founded in March 1980, by Newkirk and fellow animal rights activist Alex Pacheco, the organization first caught the public's attention in the summer of 1981 during what became known as the Silver Spring monkeys case, a widely publicized dispute about experiments conducted on 17 macaque monkeys inside the Institute of Behavioral Research in Silver Spring, Maryland. The case lasted ten years, involved the only police raid on an animal laboratory in the United States, triggered an amendment in 1985, to that country's Animal Welfare Act, and established PETA as an internationally known organization. Today it focuses on four core issues—opposition to factory farming, fur farming, animal testing, and animals in entertainment. It also campaigns against eating meat, fishing, and killing of animals regarded as pests, the keeping of chained backyard dogs, cock fighting, dog fighting, and bullfighting.

5) International Fund for Animal Welfare (IFAW)

www.ifaw.org

The International Fund for Animal Welfare (IFAW) is one of the largest animal welfare and conservation charities in the world. IFAW's mission is to rescue and protect animals around the world. The group's declared mission is to "rescue individuals, safeguard populations, and preserve habitat".

Founded in 1969, the International Fund for Animal Welfare saves individual animals, animal populations and habitats all over the world. With projects in more than 40 countries, IFAW provides hands-on assistance to animals in need, whether it's dogs and cats, wildlife and livestock, or rescuing animals in the wake of disasters. It also advocates saving populations from cruelty and depletion, such as our campaign to end commercial whaling and seal hunts.

6) The Nature Conservancy

www.nature.org

The Nature Conservancy is a charitable environmental organization, headquartered in Arlington, Virginia. Its mission is to "conserve the lands and waters on which all life depends. The Conservancy pursues non-confrontational, pragmatic solutions to conservations challenges working with partners including indigenous communities, businesses, governments, multilateral institutions, and other nonprofits.

The Conservancy's work focuses on the global priorities of Lands, Water, Climate, Oceans, and Cities. Founded in Arlington, Virginia, in 1951, The Nature Conservancy now impacts conservation in 69 countries, including all 50 states of the United States. The Conservancy has over one million members, and has protected more than 119,000,000 acres (48,000,000 ha) of land and thousands of miles of rivers worldwide. The Nature Conservancy also operates more than 100 marine conservation projects globally. The organization's assets total $6.71 billion as of 2015. The Nature Conservancy is the largest environmental nonprofit by assets and by revenue in the Americas.

7) Greenpeace International

www.greenpeace.org

Greenpeace is a non-governmental environmental organization with offices in over 40 countries and with an international coordinating body in Amsterdam, the Netherlands. Founded by Canadian and US ex-pat environmental activists in 1971, Greenpeace states its goal is to "ensure the ability of the Earth to nurture life in all its diversity" and focuses its campaigning on worldwide issues such as climate change, deforestation, overfishing, commercial whaling, genetic engineering, and anti-nuclear issues. It uses direct action, lobbying, research, and ecotage to achieve its goals. The global organization does not accept funding from governments, corporations, or political parties, relying on 2.9 million individual supporters and foundation grants. Greenpeace has a general consultative status with the United Nations Economic and Social Council and is a founding member of the INGO Accountability Charter; an international non-governmental organization that intends to foster accountability and transparency of non-governmental organizations.

8) Conservation International

www.conservation.org

Conservation International (CI) is an American nonprofit environmental organization headquartered in Arlington, Virginia. Its goal is to protect nature as a source of food, fresh water, livelihoods and a stable climate.

Conservation International was founded in 1987 with the aim of analyzing the problems most dangerous or harmful to nature and building a foundation dedicated to solving these issues on a global scale. CI's work focuses on science, policy, and partnership with businesses and communities. The organization employs more than 1,000 people and works with 2,000+ partners in more than 30 countries. CI has helped establish 1,200 protected areas across 78 countries and protected more than 730 million hectares of land, marine and coastal areas.

In CI's first year, the organization purchased a portion of Bolivia's foreign debt. The money was then redirected to support conservation in the Beni Biosphere Reserve. Since this first-ever debt-for-nature swap, more than $1 billion of similar deals have been made around the world. In 1989, CI formally committed to the protection of biodiversity hotspots, ultimately identifying 34 such hotspots around the world and contributing to their protection. The model of protecting hotspots became a key way for organizations to do conservation work.

9) Wildlife Conservation Society

www.wcs.org

WCS's goal is to conserve the world's largest wild places in 15 priority regions, home to more than 50% of the world's biodiversity. WCS saves wildlife and wild places worldwide through science, conservation action, education, and inspiring people to value nature. WCS envisions a world where wildlife thrives in healthy lands and seas, valued by societies that embrace and benefit from the diversity and integrity of life on earth.

WCS (Wildlife Conservation Society) was founded in 1895 as the New York Zoological Society (NYZS) and currently works to conserve more than two million square miles of wild places around the world. The organization is led by President and CEO Cristián Samper, former Director of the Smithsonian Institution's National Museum of Natural History. Based at the Bronx Zoo, WCS maintains approximately 500 field conservation projects in 65 countries, with 200 PhD scientists on staff. It manages four New York City wildlife parks in addition to the Bronx Zoo: the Central Park Zoo, New York Aquarium, Prospect Park Zoo and Queens Zoo. Together these parks receive 4 million visitors per year. All of the New York City facilities are accredited by the Association of Zoos and Aquariums (AZA).

10) Endangered Species International

www.endangeredspeciesinternational.org

Endangered Species International is strongly committed to reversing the trend of human-induced species extinction, saving endangered animals, and preserving wild places. Its values are - passion for nature, respect all life, integrity, optimism for solving the species extinction crisis, and progress at all levels.

11) Natural Resources Defense Council

www.nrdc.org

NRDC works to safeguard the earth—its people, its plants and animals, and the natural systems on which all life depends.

The Natural Resources Defense Council (NRDC) is a New York City-based, nonprofit international environmental advocacy group, with offices in New York City, Washington, D.C., San Francisco, Los Angeles, Chicago, Bozeman, Montana, and Beijing, China. Founded in 1970, NRDC today has 2.4 million members and online activities nationwide and a staff of about 500 lawyers, scientists and other policy advocates across the globe to ensure the rights of all people to the air, the water, and the wild. The charity monitoring group Charity Navigator gave the Natural Resources Defense Council four out of four stars in its three rating categories: overall, financial practices, and accountability & transparency.

12) Friends of the Earth International (FoEI)

www.foei.org

Friends of the Earth was founded in 1969 as an anti-nuclear group by Robert O Anderson who contributed $200,000 in personal funds to launch FOTE with David Brower, Donald Aitken and Jerry Mander after Brower's split with the Sierra Club. FOTE main mission was to lock up and prevent further development of nuclear energy. It is the world's largest grassroots environmental network, uniting 75 national member groups and some 5,000 local activist groups on every continent. With over 2 million members and supporters around the world, it campaigns on today's most urgent environmental and social issues. It challenges the current model of economic and corporate globalization, and promotes solutions that will help to create environmentally sustainable and socially just societies.

13) World Vets

www.worldvets.org

World Vets' Mission is to improve the health and wellbeing of animals by providing veterinary aid and training in developing countries and by providing disaster relief worldwide. World Vets vision is to create a world where all animals have access to skilled veterinary care. Its programs span 45 countries on 6 continents. It works in partnership with animal welfare groups, foreign governments, non-governmental organizations, agriculture and public health officials, as well as, a wide variety of veterinary professionals in the countries where we provide service. World Vets is able to improve the lives of thousands of animals each year by providing free veterinary care through our dedicated volunteer force of over 4,000 individuals combined with financial support and in-kind donations.

14) Biosphere Expeditions

www.biosphere-expeditions.org

Biosphere Expeditions is a wildlife research and conservation nonprofit organization whose main focus is to conserve the biosphere with volunteer-led scientific conservation expeditions to several countries around the world. It was founded in 1999. Biosphere Expeditions states its purpose as the promotion of sustainable conservation of the planet's wildlife by involving the public, with scientists across the globe on real hands-on wildlife research and conservation expeditions. Expeditions typically place interested people with no research experience alongside scientists widely accepted to be at the forefront of their conservation work. Anyone may join an expedition as there are neither special skills or fitness requirements nor age limitations. Biosphere Expeditions promotes sustainable conservation and preservation of the planet's wildlife by forging alliances between scientists and the public.

15) Environmental Defense Fund

www.edf.org

Environmental Defense Fund or EDF (formerly known as Environmental Defense) is a United States–based nonprofit environmental advocacy group. The group is known for its work on issues including global warming, ecosystem restoration, oceans, and human health, and advocates using sound science, economics and law to find environmental solutions that work. It is nonpartisan, and its work often advocates market-based solutions to environmental problems.

It is one of the world's largest environmental organizations, with more than 1.5 million members and a staff of 550 scientists, economists, policy experts, and other professionals around the world. It believes prosperity and environmental stewardship must go hand in hand. It is an optimist because it has seen its ideas make a huge difference. And it builds strong partnerships across interests to ensure lasting success. It achieves results by finding solutions that benefit people while protecting natural systems.

16) Oceana

www.oceana.org

Oceana seeks to make our oceans as rich, healthy, and abundant as they once were. Oceana seeks to make our oceans more biodiverse and abundant by winning policy victories in the countries that govern much of the world's marine life.

Oceana was established in 2001 by a group of leading foundations — The Pew Charitable Trusts, Oak Foundation, Marisla Foundation (formerly Homeland Foundation), and the Rockefeller Brothers Fund. It is an international organization focused solely on oceans, dedicated to achieving measurable change by conducting specific, science-based campaigns with fixed deadlines and articulated goals. Oceana was created to identify practical solutions and make them happen. Since its founding, Oceana has won more than 100 victories and protected more than 1.2 million square miles of ocean.

17) Coral Reef Alliance

www.coral.org

CORAL promotes conservation through its Coral Reef Sustainable Destination (CRSD) approach, a holistic model that combines marine protected area (MPA) management and sustainable business operation for community benefit.

The Coral Reef Alliance (CORAL) is a nonprofit organization based in San Francisco, California, which partners with local reef communities around the world to protect coral reefs. CORAL was founded in Berkeley,

California, in 1994 by Stephen Colwell, and is currently headed by Dr. Michael Webster. With 19% of the world's coral reefs already destroyed and another 35% at immediate risk or threatened due to human pressures, organizations like CORAL are addressing an urgent need.

The organization was founded in 1994 by Stephen Colwell in Berkeley, California. In the beginning, the goal was simple: to engage the diving community in coral reef conservation. Today, CORAL's mission of uniting communities to save coral reefs has dramatically broadened the scope of its work and has provided extensive opportunities to have an even greater impact around the globe.

18) Wildlife Conservation Network

www.wildnet.org

The Wildlife Conservation Network (WCN) is a United States-based 501(c) (3) nonprofit organization whose mission is to protect endangered species and preserve their natural habitats by supporting entrepreneurial conservationists who pursue innovative strategies for people and wildlife to co-exist and thrive.

WCN was built on the premise that one person can truly make a difference for wildlife. Independent wildlife conservationists have the power to ensure a future for wildlife by developing new solutions and working closely with communities to save endangered animals. In order to succeed, these wildlife heroes need funding to run their programs and assistance to build their organizations and ensure their efforts are scalable and sustainable. WCN partners with leading independent wildlife conservationists, providing them with an array of services and training in areas such as marketing, accounting, and strategic planning. WCN also creates connections to donors who can make these conservationists' work possible.

19) Rainforest Alliance

www.rainforest-alliance.org

The Rainforest Alliance is a non-governmental organization (NGO) working to conserve biodiversity and ensure sustainable livelihoods by transforming land-use practices, business practices and consumer behavior. Based in New York City with offices throughout North and South America, Asia, Africa and Europe, it was founded in 1987 by Daniel Katz, who serves on its board of directors, and is led by President Nigel Sizer. The Rainforest Alliance is a growing network of people who are inspired and committed to working together to achieve our mission of conserving biodiversity and ensuring sustainable livelihoods. Through creative, pragmatic collaboration, we aim to rebalance the planet by building strong forests and healthy communities around the world.

The Rainforest Alliance's talented, multilingual, and diverse staff works hand-in-hand around the world with farmers, foresters, businesses, researchers, civic organizations, and governments to meet our shared mission of conserving biodiversity and ensuring sustainable livelihoods. From its earliest days in the tropics of Central America, it has grown its alliance by partnering with forest and farming communities, governments, and companies to conserve critically important forests and cultivate sustainable livelihoods. Today, it conducts training, certification, and verification in 74 countries around the world.

20) World Animal Protection

www.worldanimalprotection.org

World Animal Protection (formerly The World Society for the Protection of Animals) is an international nonprofit animal welfare organization that has been in operation for over 30 years. The charity describes its vision as: A world where animal welfare matters and animal cruelty has ended. *"We end the needless suffering of animals. We influence decision makers to put animals on the global agenda. We help the world see how important animals are to all of us. We inspire people to change animals' lives for the better. We move the world to protect animals."* The charity has regional hubs in: Africa, Asia, Europe, Latin America and North America, and offices in 14 countries. The international office is in London.

The organization was previously known as the World Society for the Protection of Animals (WSPA). This resulted from the merger of two animal welfare organizations in 1981, the World Federation for the Protection of Animals (WFPA) founded in 1953 and the International Society for the Protection of Animals (ISPA) founded in 1959. In June 2014, the charity became World Animal Protection, at a cost of £168,000.

21) Last Chance for Animals (LCA)

www.lcanimal.org

Last Chance for Animals (LCA) is a US nonprofit organization that advocates for animal rights. It is known for its documentary, Dealing Dogs, and for its investigations against the use of animals for testing purposes. The organization was founded in 1984 by Hollywood actor Chris DeRose as a group to oppose vivisection. In the organization's early years, DeRose led teams of activists employing non-violent strategies modeled after social movements led by such leaders as Mahatma Gandhi and Martin Luther King, Jr. Last Chance for Animals seeks to eliminate animal exploitation through direct action, education, investigations, legislation, and media attention. LCA opposes the use of animals in food and clothing production, scientific experimentation, and entertainment. LCA also promotes a cruelty-free lifestyle and the ascription of rights to non-human beings. They support veganism and oppose animal testing.

22) Defenders of Wildlife

www.defenders.org

Defenders of Wildlife is a 501(c) (3) nonprofit conservation organization based in the United States. Its mission is to protect all animals and plants native to North America in their natural communities. Founded in 1947, Defenders of Wildlife is a major national conservation organization dedicated to conserving wildlife, protecting their natural habitats, and safeguarding biodiversity. Operationally, Defenders of Wildlife has a three-pronged approach:

On the ground at the state and local level, Defenders is involved in developing programs that protect and restore key species and habitats.

Defenders works with state, national, and international policy makers to secure laws and policies that protect animals and their habitats.

Defenders is active in the courts establishing legal safeguards for native wildlife and fighting efforts to roll back environmental protections.

23) Center for Biological Diversity

www.biologicaldiversity.org

The Center for Biological Diversity (Center), based in Tucson, Arizona, is a nonprofit membership organization with approximately 1.1 million members and online activists, known for its work protecting endangered species through legal action, scientific petitions, creative media and grassroots activism. The Center has offices and staff in New Mexico, Arizona, Nevada, California, Oregon, Illinois, Minnesota, Alaska, Vermont, Florida and Washington, D.C. It was founded in 1989 by Kieran Suckling, Peter Galvin, Todd Schulke and Robin Silver. Given a small grant by the Fund for Wild Nature, the organization started in 1989 as a small group by the name of Greater Gila Biodiversity Project, with the objective to protect endangered species and critical habitat in the southwest. The organization later grew and became the Center for Biological Diversity.

24) Sierra Club

www.sierraclub.org

The Sierra Club is an environmental organization in the United States. It was founded on May 28, 1892, in San Francisco, California, by the Scottish-American preservationist John Muir, who became its first president. The Sierra Club's stated mission is "To explore, enjoy, and protect the wild places of the earth; to practice and promote the responsible use of the earth's ecosystems and resources; to educate and enlist humanity to protect and restore the quality of the natural and human environment; and to use all lawful means to carry out these objectives."

Traditionally associated with the progressive movement, the club was one of the first large-scale environmental preservation organizations in the world, and currently engages in lobbying politicians to promote green policies. In recent years, the club has gravitated toward green politics and especially toward bright green environmentalism. Recent focuses of the club include promoting green energy, mitigating global warming, and opposing coal.

25) EARTHJUSTICE

www.earthjustice.org

Earthjustice is a nonprofit public interest law organization based in the United States dedicated to environmental issues. It is headquartered in San

Francisco, has nine regional offices across the United States, an international department, a communications team, and a policy team in Washington, DC. Earthjustice's work is divided into three major program areas:

- Health and Toxics – focuses on cases that fight for healthy communities.

- Climate and Energy – focuses on cases that advance clean energy and promote a stable climate.

- The Wild – focuses on cases that preserve our wildlife and wild lands.

Earthjustice also partners with organizations from other regions, including Latin America, Russia, Japan, and China to promote the development of environmental law in their respective countries. Every year, Earthjustice submits a country-by-country report on Human Rights and the Environment to the United Nations.

Earthjustice is a nonprofit and does not charge any of its clients for its services. Funding for the organization comes from individual donations and foundations. It does not receive any funding from corporations or governments. The organization was founded in 1971 as the Sierra Club Legal Defense Fund, though it was fully independent from the Sierra Club. It changed its name to Earthjustice in 1997 to better reflect its role as a legal advocate representing hundreds of regional, national and international organizations. As of January 2009, the group had provided free legal representation to more than 700 clients ranging from the Sierra Club, World Wildlife Fund, and the American Lung Association to smaller state and community groups, such as the Maine Lobstermen's Association and the Friends of the Everglades.

26) Ocean Conservancy

www.oceanconservancy.org

Ocean Conservancy (founded as The Delta Corporation) is a nonprofit environmental advocacy group based in Washington, D.C., United States. The organization helps formulate ocean policy at the federal and state government levels based on peer reviewed science. Ocean Conservancy is one of the few organizations that help protect wildlife in the ocean.

Ocean Conservancy was founded in 1972, as the Delta Corporation to promote healthy and diverse ocean ecosystems, and to oppose practices that threaten oceanic and human life. Through several program areas,

Ocean Conservancy advocates for protecting of special marine habitats, restoring sustainable fisheries, reducing the human impact on ocean ecosystems and managing U.S. ocean resources. Ocean Conservancy efforts are guided by a 17-member volunteer board of directors. Ocean Conservancy is a tax-exempt not-for-profit organization. It meets the Better Business Bureau's 20 Standards for Charity Accountability.

27) Global Coral Reef Alliance

www.globalcoral.org

The Global Coral Reef Alliance is a small, 501(c)(3) nonprofit organization dedicated to growing, protecting and managing the most threatened of all marine ecosystems—coral reefs. Founded in 1990, GCRA is a coalition of volunteer scientists, divers, environmentalists and other individuals and organizations, committed to coral reef preservation. We primarily focus on coral reef restoration, marine diseases and other issues caused by global climate change, environmental stress and pollution.

GCRA scientists work with foundations, governments or private firms to build, restore and maintain coral reefs, nurseries and marine sanctuaries. Projects include restoration and construction of coral reefs for mariculture and tourism as well as breakwaters for shore protection.

28) Project AWARE

www.projectaware.org

Project AWARE is a registered nonprofit organization working with volunteer scuba divers. With offices in UK, US and Australia, Project AWARE supports divers acting in their own communities to protect the ocean, with a focus on implementing lasting change in two core areas: shark conservation and marine litter.

In 1989, the Professional Association of Diving Instructors (PADI) established the Project AWARE Foundation. By 2008, it had become one of the largest (by geographical coverage) of several 'industry led' environmental organizations, with administration offices in the United States, United Kingdom, Australia, Switzerland and Japan. In 1992, Project AWARE Foundation became a registered nonprofit organization with an environmental mission and purpose. Project AWARE relaunched as a movement in 2011 to help divers in more than 180 countries to work together for a clean, healthy and abundant ocean.

29) African Wildlife Foundation

www.awf.org

The African Wildlife Foundation, together with the people of Africa, works to ensure the wildlife and wild lands of Africa will endure forever. AWF's programs and conservation strategies are designed to protect the wildlife and wild lands of Africa and ensure a more sustainable future for Africa's people. AWF stops the degradation of animals and the world's environment.

The African Wildlife Foundation (AWF), founded in 1961 as the African Wildlife Leadership Foundation, is an international conservation organization that focuses on critically important landscapes in Africa. Since its inception, the organization has protected endangered species and land, promoted conservation enterprises that benefit local African communities, and trained hundreds of African nationals in conservation— all to ensure the survival of Africa's unparalleled wildlife heritage.

30) Wildlife Trust of India

www.wti.org.in

Wildlife Trust of India (WTI) is a leading Indian nature conservation organization committed to the service of nature. Its mission is to conserve wildlife and its habitat and to work for the welfare of individual wild animals, in partnership with communities and governments. WTI's team of 150 dedicated professionals work towards achieving its vision of a secure natural heritage of India, in six priority landscapes, knit holistically together by seven key strategies or Big Ideas.

WTI was formed in November 1998 in response to the rapidly deteriorating condition of wildlife in India. It currently focuses its resources on six priority landscapes – northeast India, western Himalayas, terai, southern Ghats system, central India and marine.

31) Nature Conservation Foundation

www.ncf-india.org

The Nature Conservation Foundation is a non-governmental wildlife conservation and research organization based in Mysore, India. They promote the use of science for wildlife conservation in India. The organization was founded in 1996. Their mission is to carry out "science-based and socially responsible conservation".

The organization works in a variety of habitats. The high altitude program focuses on human wildlife conflicts and conservation of endangered species such as the snow leopard and the Tibetan gazelle. It has partnered with the International Snow Leopard Trust and the Government of India to launch a Project Snow Leopard, similar to Project Tiger for the protection of the wildlife in the Himalayan landscapes. It runs a rainforest restoration program in the Annamalai hills in the Western Ghats where fragments of degraded patches of rainforests outside national parks or wildlife sanctuaries are restored in partnership with the private tea and coffee plantations.

32) In Defense of Animals

www.idausa.org

Founded in 1983 by Dr. Elliot Katz DVM in San Rafael, California, USA, In Defense of Animals is an international animal rights and rescue organization dedicated to protecting the rights, welfare and habitats of animals. It has 60,000 members and an annual budget of $650,000. The group's slogan is "working to protect the rights, welfare, and habitats of animals". IDA has become known, in particular, for its campaigns against animal experiments conducted by the U.S. military, and experiments in which baby monkeys are separated from their mothers. Journalist and author Deborah Blum has described its strategy as "pure pit bull. It picks a target carefully and refuses to let go".

"We are supported by a network of tens of thousands of determined activists, dedicated volunteers, interns and donors. We work to expose and end animal experimentation; protect wildlife and restore balance in their natural habitats; end the exploitation and abuse of wild species living in captivity, protect domestic and wild species worldwide from abuse and slaughter for food, conduct cruelty investigations and rescue operations, and provide veterinary care for sick, abused and orphaned animals in our natural habitat sanctuaries."

IDA Africa was founded by former Portland, Oregon veterinarian Dr. Sheri Speede, the Center provides sanctuary for chimpanzee orphans in Cameroon, while promoting social and cultural conditions that ensure that endangered great apes survive and thrive in their natural habitats. To help ensure the survival of chimpanzees orphaned by the illegal ape meat trade, our Sanaga-Yong Chimpanzee Rescue Center currently cares for 72 orphaned chimpanzees in a forested habitat.

IDA INDIA is a nonprofit grassroots-level animal protection organization, dedicated to establishing and defending the rights of all non–human living creatures. In Defense of Animals, India was established on 31st October 1996. Immediately the project of neutering of street dogs was taken up. A small beginning was made in March 1997 in two garages of a residential colony in a suburb of Mumbai. For three years IDA INDIA worked in small make shift camps. With the intervention of the Mumbai High Court, the Corporation handed over the premises at Deonar to IDA INDIA on 22nd December 1999.

33) Mercy for Animals

www.mercyforanimals.org

Mercy For Animals (MFA) is an international nonprofit organization dedicated to preventing cruelty to farmed animals and promoting compassionate food choices and policies, founded in October 1999. Nathan Runkle is the group's executive director and founder. Focusing primarily on advocacy on behalf of farmed animals, MFA runs a number of campaigns that aim to educate the public on animal protection issues and to encourage them to adopt a vegan diet. It has engaged in several undercover investigations, primarily of egg farms, and has produced television commercials showing the treatment of animals in slaughterhouses and factory farms. They have offices in Los Angeles, Chicago, New York City, Ohio, Texas, and Toronto. MFA's national headquarters is located in Los Angeles. Mercy for Animals is currently one of Animal Charity Evaluators' Top Charities.

34) Animal Legal Defense Fund (ALDF)

www.aldf.org

The Animal Legal Defense Fund's mission is to protect the lives and advance the interests of animals through the legal system. ALDF accomplishes this mission by filing high-impact lawsuits to protect animals from harm, providing free legal assistance and training to prosecutors to assure that animal abusers are punished for their crimes, supporting tough animal protection legislation and fighting harmful animal protection legislation, and providing resources and opportunities to law students and professionals to advance the emerging field of animal law.

Founded in 1979 by attorneys active in shaping the emerging field of animal law, ALDF has blazed the trail for stronger enforcement of anti-cruelty laws and more humane treatment of animals in every corner of American life. Today, ALDF's groundbreaking efforts to push the U.S. legal system to end the suffering of abused animals are supported by thousands of dedicated attorneys and more than 200,000 members and supporters.

35) Humane Society International (HSI)

www.hsi.org

Humane Society International is one of the only global animal protection organizations working to help all animals—including animals in laboratories, animals on farms, companion animals and wildlife— and our record of achievement demonstrates our dedication and effectiveness. HSI: Celebrating Animals, Confronting Cruelty. Humane Society International (HSI) is the international division of The Humane Society of the United States. Founded in 1991, HSI has expanded The HSUS's activities into Central and South America, Africa, and Asia. HSI's Asian, Australian, Canadian, and European offices carry out field activities and programs.

36) 350.org

www.350.org

350.org is an international environmental organization encouraging citizens to action with the belief that publicizing the increasing levels of carbon dioxide will pressure world leaders to address climate change and to reduce levels from 400 parts per million to 350 parts per million. It was founded by author Bill McKibben with the goal of building a global grassroots movement to raise awareness about human-driven climate change, to confront climate change denial, and to cut emissions of carbon dioxide in order to slow the rate of global warming. 350.org takes its name from the research of Goddard Institute for Space Studies scientist James E. Hansen, who posited in a 2007 paper that 350 parts-per-million (ppm) of CO_2 in the atmosphere is a safe upper limit to avoid a climate tipping point.

37) Alliance for International Reforestation

www.airguatemala.org

Alliance for International Reforestation is a nonprofit improving human and environmental health in Guatemala. Over 2,800 farm families trained, 840+ efficient stoves built, and 4.8 million trees planted and counting! For over 22 years, it has implemented our community based 5 year approach with great results and success. It employs local professionals, use native trees and materials, build custom stoves and train farmers on their own land.

38) American Society for the Prevention of Cruelty to Animals (ASPCA)

www.aspca.org

The American Society for the Prevention of Cruelty to Animals (ASPCA) is a nonprofit organization dedicated to preventing cruelty to animals. It was the first humane society to be established in North America and is, today, one of the largest in the world with more than 2 million supporters across the country. Based in New York City since its inception in 1866, the organization's mission is "to provide effective means for the prevention of cruelty to animals throughout the United States". It was founded on the belief that animals are entitled to kind and respectful treatment at the hands of humans and must be protected under the law.

39) Amazon Conservation Association (ACA)

www.amazonconservation.org

Its mission is to protect the world's most diverse landscapes, train the next generation of Amazonian conservationists, and partner with communities to support livelihoods that sustain biodiversity. It is working to conserve the biodiversity of the Amazon basin through the development of new scientific understanding, sustainable resource management and rational land-use policy. A principal objective of the organization is to develop field research sites ranging from high elevation cloud forest to the lowland Amazon. It is this altitudinal gradient that harbors the greatest known richness of species on the planet. At the ACA field sites, university students and researchers are brought to study and observe this diverse ecosystem.

40) Best Friends Animal Society

www.bestfriends.org

Best Friends Animal Society, founded in its present form in 1991, is an American nonprofit 501(c) (3) animal welfare organization. Best Friends works nationwide in outreach programs with shelters, rescue groups and members to promote pet adoption, no-kill animal rescue, and spay-and-neuter practices. The mission of Best Friends Animal Society is to bring about a time when there are No More Homeless Pets. It does this by helping end the killing in America's animal shelters through building community programs and partnerships all across the nation. *"We believe that by working together we can Save Them All"*.

41) Big Life Foundation

www.biglife.org

Big Life was co-founded by photographer Nick Brandt and award-winning conservationist Richard Bonham in September 2010. Since its inception, Big Life has expanded to employ hundreds of Maasai rangers—with more than 40 permanent outposts and tent-based field units, 13 vehicles, tracker dogs, and aerial surveillance—protecting 2 million acres of wilderness in the Amboseli-Tsavo-Kilimanjaro ecosystem of East Africa. Big Life was the first organization in East Africa to establish coordinated cross-border anti-poaching operations. Using innovative conservation strategies and collaborating closely with local communities, partner NGOs, national parks, and government agencies, Big Life seeks to protect and sustain East Africa's wildlife and wild lands, including one of the greatest populations of elephants left in East Africa.

42) Blind Cat Rescue & Sanctuary

www.blindcatrescue.com

A lifetime cat care sanctuary located in St. Pauls, North Carolina (USA). In 2005, it built its first building as a safe place for blind cats who were deemed not adoptable by regular shelters and who were going to be euthanized just because they were blind. In 2011, it built a second shelter to provide a safe place for Leukemia positive (FELV+) and Feline Immunodeficiency Virus (FIV+) cats who otherwise would have been killed just because they tested positive for those viruses.

43) Environmental Law Alliance Worldwide (ELAW)

www.elaw.org

The Environmental Law Alliance Worldwide (ELAW) helps communities speak out for clean air, clean water, and a healthy planet. We are a global alliance of attorneys, scientists and other advocates collaborating across borders to promote grassroots efforts to build a sustainable, just future. ELAW advocates, working in their home countries, know best how to protect the environment. By giving our partners the legal and scientific support they need, ELAW helps challenge environmental abuses and builds a worldwide corps of skilled, committed advocates working to protect ecosystems and communities for generations to come.

44) Hope for Paws

www.hopeforpaws.org

Hope for Paws was created to help animals who suffer and die every year because of negligence and abuse. It is a nonprofit animal rescue organization which rescues dogs and all other animals who are suffering on the streets and in the shelters. Its goal is to educate people on the importance of companion animals in the society.

45) National Audubon Society

www.audubon.org

The National Audubon Society (Audubon) is a nonprofit environmental organization dedicated to conservation. Audubon's mission is to conserve and restore natural ecosystems, focusing on birds, other wildlife, and their habitats for the benefit of humanity and the earth's biological diversity. Located in the United States and incorporated in 1905, it is one of the oldest of such organizations in the world and uses science, education and grassroots advocacy to advance its conservation mission. The society's main offices are in New York City and Washington, D.C., and it has state offices in about 24 states. It also owns and operates a number of nature centers open to the public, located in urban settings, including New York City, Joplin, Phoenix, Dallas, and Los Angeles, as well as at bird refuges and other natural areas. Audubon Centers help to forge lifelong connections between people and nature, developing stewards for conservation among young and diverse communities.

46) National Wildlife Federation

www.nwf.org

National Wildlife Federation (NWF) is a voice for wildlife, dedicated to protecting wildlife and habitat and inspiring the future generation of conservationists. It is the United States' largest private, nonprofit conservation education and advocacy organization, with over six million members and supporters, and 51 state and territorial affiliated organizations (including Puerto Rico and the Virgin Islands). The NWF strives to remain "A national network of like-minded state and territorial groups, seeking balanced, common-sense solutions to environmental problems that work for wildlife and people".

47) Ocean Defenders Alliance

www.oceandefenders.org

Founded in 2000 and based in Orange County, California, Ocean Defenders Alliance (ODA) is a marine conservation organization which works to clean and protect marine ecosystems through documentation, education, and meaningful action. Working with affected communities, we focus primarily on the reduction and removal of man-made debris which poses serious threats to ocean wildlife and habitats. In addition to doing invaluable work at sea, ODA also works onshore to educate the public about the vital need for clean and healthy oceans. Through educational presentations at schools, expos, festivals, and dive clubs, we strive to inform people of all types and ages, raise their awareness about the plight of the oceans, and inspire them to join our efforts. ODA also reaches out to fishermen, restaurants, and the seafood community to enlighten them to these issues and seek to gain their commitment to becoming better stewards of the oceans.

48) Oil Change International

www.priceofoil.org

Oil Change International is a research, communication, and advocacy organization focused on exposing the true costs of fossil fuels and facilitating the coming transition towards clean energy. We focus on the fossil fuel industry because we view the production and consumption of oil, gas and coal as sources of global warming, human rights abuses, war, national security concerns, corporate globalization, and increased inequality. We also see fossil fuel industry's interests behind every major barrier to a clean energy transition.

49) Pandas International

www.pandasinternational.org

The Giant Panda, one of the most delightful and captivating of animals, is also one of the most endangered. The best scientific estimates indicate that there are less than 2,200 Giant Pandas remaining in the world today. Pandas International is a registered nonprofit organization which helps save this magnificent animal. Unlike other organizations which serve many animals, Pandas International is exclusively devoted to the Giant Panda. The mission of Pandas International is to ensure the preservation and propagation of the endangered Giant Panda. It provides public awareness and education, support for research, habitat preservation and enhancement, and assistance to Giant Panda Centers.

50) Paws Animal Wildlife Sanctuary

www.paws-sc.com

Paws Animal Wildlife Sanctuary, Inc. (PAWS) is an all-volunteer nonprofit organization focusing on wildlife education, rescue and rehabilitation. It operates out of South Carolina and carries rehabilitation permits from the state and federal government, as well as USDA and USFWS permits for legal public display of resident animals in wildlife education programs. Its mission is to rescue, rehabilitate, and release orphaned or injured wildlife, and to provide educational live-animal presentations that promote peaceful coexistence with native North American wildlife.

51) Plant & Animals Welfare Society (PAWS)

www.pawsmumbai.org

Plant & Animals Welfare Society – Mumbai (PAWS-Mumbai) is an independently registered Non-Government Organization (NGO) founded in 2002 by like-minded youth who love to work in the field of animal welfare and environment protection under the leadership of young animal lover & environment friend Sunish Subramanian Kunju. The youth believed that their consistent efforts at grass-root level would be able to bring about a change on the two fronts. Over the years we have raised several pertinent issues concerning the environment and animals.

52) Rainforest Partnership

www.rainforestpartnership.org

"We envision thriving tropical rainforests that support a healthy, vibrant planet."

Its mission is to protect and regenerate tropical rainforests by working with the people of the forests to develop sustainable livelihoods that empower and respect both people and nature. Rainforest Partnership is an impact and data driven international nonprofit dedicated to protecting tropical rainforests, the lungs of our planet and a critical factor in its health.

The Amazon Basin alone stores 400 million metric tons of CO_2 per year – about 25% of all carbon stored on land and it produces 20% of the world's oxygen. Nearly 4,500 acres of rainforests are lost every hour from illegal logging, mining, agriculture, forest fires, and oil drilling, resulting in a lot more carbon in the atmosphere – and a lot less oxygen. Rainforest Partnership works directly with rainforest communities to sustainably develop products found in the forest, giving the community a stake in keeping their trees intact.

53) RedRover

www.redrover.org

Founded in 1987, the mission of RedRover is to bring animals out of crisis and strengthen the bond between people and animals through emergency sheltering, disaster relief services, financial assistance and education. RedRover accomplishes its mission by engaging volunteers and supporters, collaborating with others and maximizing the use of online technology. RedRover is a soft hand and warm heart in times when animals and people are in need, crisis and pain. It brings animals out of crisis and into care, and discovers new ways to strengthen the common bond between people and animals.

54) Stop Animal Exploitation Now! (SAEN)

www.saenonline.org | www.all-creatures.org/saen

Stop Animal Exploitation NOW! (SAEN) was founded in 1996 to force an end to the abuse of animals in laboratories. Our first major event was a news conference that revealed the suffering endured by dogs, rabbits, and primates in 9 laboratories across the United States.

Since its inception, SAEN staff and the tireless volunteers who support our campaigns on the local level have allowed us to make a real difference for the animals. With the help of grassroots activists, SAEN has ended pound seizure (the sale of former pets from animal shelters to labs) in Nashville (TN), and we have also ended abusive experiments on primates in San Diego (CA). In its brief history, SAEN has made a concrete difference for the animals, and it will continue to fight for their freedom until all the laboratory cages are empty.

55) The Humane Society of the United States

www.humanesociety.org

The Humane Society of the United States is the nation's largest and most effective animal protection organization. The organization and its affiliates provide hands-on care and services to more than 100,000 animals each year, and professionalizes the field through education and training for local organizations. We are the leading animal advocacy organization, seeking a humane world for people and animals alike. The organization is driving transformational change in the U.S. and around the world by combating large-scale cruelties such as puppy mills, animal fighting, factory farming, seal slaughter, horse cruelty, captive hunts and the wildlife trade.

56) The Wild Animal Sanctuary

www.wildanimalsanctuary.org

The Wild Animal Sanctuary is a 720-acre (290 ha) animal sanctuary located near Keenesburg, Colorado, United States. The sanctuary specializes in rescuing and caring for large predators which are being ill-treated, for which their owners can no longer care, or which might otherwise be euthanized. Created in 1980, The Wild Animal Sanctuary is situated on grassland North of Denver, and has helped over 1,000 animals since it first opened. As of 2013, it was home to over 330 animals.

The stated mission of the sanctuary is "to rescue captive large carnivores who have been abused, abandoned, illegally kept or exploited; to create for them a wonderful life for as long as they live; and to educate about the causes and solutions to the Captive Wildlife Crisis." The sanctuary states that there are many large carnivores living outside the zoo system in the United States, including 4000 or so tigers living as pets in Texas alone, and many of these come from the black market trade in exotic animals.

57) Voices for Biodiversity

www.voicesforbiodiversity.org

"Voices for Biodiversity" is a participatory online magazine that educates and raises awareness about the biodiversity crisis by sharing stories and building a community around story-sharing. Voices for Biodiversity is a conservation-oriented nonprofit that connects people from around the world to protect biodiversity. V4B's e-zine (electronic magazine) builds a community around global story-sharing and creates a gathering place for those who believe humanity's health and wellbeing depend upon the health and wellbeing of other species. "Voices for Biodiversity" focuses on sharing the voices of those who usually would not be heard: indigenous and local peoples, students, non-experts, and more. Anyone can submit content and be published.

58) World Animal Awareness Society

www.wa2s.org

The World Animal Awareness Society & WA2S Films create innovative social programs and produce cutting edge viral videos about human - animal interaction. Animal welfare nonprofits and communities benefit directly from innovative programming custom produced to each specific subject.

59) Tree Roo Rescue and Conservation Centre Ltd.

www.treeroorescue.org.au

It is a nonprofit organization that rescues and rehabilitates, orphaned, injured or displaced tree kangaroos for release back into the wild or for life in captivity as breeding animals for education and conservation in Zoos. It also wish to educate the public and increase awareness of Australian tree kangaroo conservation and the threats that bring them into care such as dogs and cars. Its Vision is to assist in the prevention of the extinction of Tree kangaroos.

60) The United Nations Children's Fund (UNICEF)

www.unicef.org

The United Nations Children's Fund is a United Nations programme headquartered in New York City that provides humanitarian and developmental assistance to children and mothers in developing countries. UNICEF works in 190 countries and territories to protect the rights of every child. UNICEF has spent 70 years working to improve the lives of children and their families. Defending children's rights throughout their lives requires a global presence, aiming to produce results and understand their effects. UNICEF believes - All children have a right to survive, thrive and fulfill their potential – to the benefit of a better world. For 70 years, UNICEF has worked to improve the lives of children and their families. Despite remarkable challenges around the world, UNICEF staffers fight for the rights of every child seeking safe shelter, nutrition, protection from disaster and conflicts, and equality. UNICEF works with the United Nations other United Nations agencies to make sure that children are on the global agenda. UNICEF strikes a balance between thorough research and practical solutions for children.

61) Wikimedia Foundation

www.wikimediafoundation.org

The Wikimedia Foundation, Inc. is a nonprofit charitable organization dedicated to encouraging the growth, development and distribution of free, multilingual, educational content, and to providing the full content of these wiki-based projects to the public free of charge. The Wikimedia Foundation operates some of the largest collaboratively edited reference projects in the world, including **Wikipedia**, a top-ten internet property. *Imagine a world in which every single human being can freely share in the sum of all knowledge.* That's their commitment. The Wikimedia Foundation relies heavily on the generous support from its users. Please consider making a donation today, be it time or money. Wikipedia is the world's largest free encyclopedia available to everyone who has access to the internet. There is hardly any topic on which Wikipedia doesn't have the information. It is the largest free source of knowledge. Hence, all must support the organization behind, which has been operating these kinds of giant projects for its entire life. Other projects include – Wiktionary (Dictionary and Thesaurus), Wikinews (Free Content News Source), Wikibooks (Free Text Books and Manuals), Wikiquote (Collection of

Quotations), Wikisource (Free Source Documents), Wikiversity (Free Learning Tools), Wikivoyage (Free Travel Guide), Wikispecies (Directory of Species), Commons (Shared Media Repository), Wikidata (Free Knowledge Base), Mediawiki (Free Wiki Software).

The Rest of the Organizations – How to find them?

The rest of the organizations if not all, at least most of them can be found on the websites of **GreatNonprofits** and **CharityWatch**.

GreatNonprofits (www.greatnonprofits.org) — is the leading platform for community-sourced stories about Nonprofits. These stories are submitted by people who know the best about the organizations – their clients, donors, volunteers, and others – all those who have experienced the impact of nonprofit work up close.

CharityWatch (www.charitywatch.org) — founded more than 20 years ago as the American Institute of Philanthropy (AIP)—is America's most independent, assertive charity watchdog. CharityWatch does not merely repeat what a charity reports using simplistic or automated formulas. It dives deep to let people know how efficiently a charity will use their donation to fund the programs they want to support. CharityWatch exposes nonprofit abuses and advocates for your interests as a donor.

Global Warming and Climate Change

The information mentioned here comes directly from NASA and what its scientists have to say on the topic of global warming. It also contains relevant evidence which can be found on its website. I highly recommend you to have a look at it by visiting www.climate.nasa.gov. That will help you know better what exactly is going on around the world and how badly the environment has been affected.

"Climate change" and "global warming" are often used interchangeably but have distinct meanings. Similarly, the terms "weather" and "climate" are sometimes confused, though they refer to events with broadly different locations and timescales.

Weather refers to atmospheric conditions that occur locally over short periods of time - from minutes to hours or days. Familiar examples include rain, snow, clouds, winds, floods or thunderstorms. Remember, weather is local and short-term.

Climate, on the other hand, refers to the long-term regional or even global average of temperature, humidity and rainfall patterns over seasons, years or decades. Remember, climate is global and long-term.

Global warming refers to the upward temperature trend across the entire Earth since the early 20th century, and most notably since the late 1970s, due to the increase in fossil fuel emissions since the industrial revolution. Worldwide since 1880, the average surface temperature has gone up by about 0.8 °C (1.4 °F), relative to the mid-20th-century baseline (of 1951-1980).

Climate change refers to a broad range of global phenomena created predominantly by burning fossil fuels, which add heat-trapping gases to Earth's atmosphere. These phenomena include the increased temperature trends described by global warming, but also encompass changes such as sea level rise; ice mass loss in Greenland, Antarctica, the Arctic and mountain glaciers worldwide; shifts in flower/plant blooming; and extreme weather events.

The Earth's climate has changed throughout history. In the last 650,000 years alone, there have been seven cycles of glacial advance and retreat,

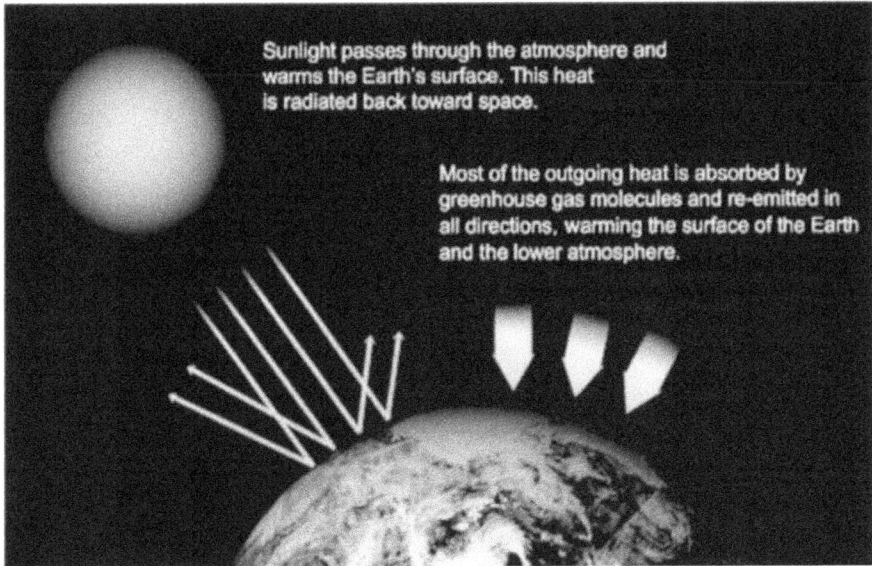

Sunlight passes through the atmosphere and warms the Earth's surface. This heat is radiated back toward space.

Most of the outgoing heat is absorbed by greenhouse gas molecules and re-emitted in all directions, warming the surface of the Earth and the lower atmosphere.

Greenhouse Effect
(Source : NASA)

with the abrupt end of the last ice age about 7,000 years ago marking the beginning of the modern climate era — and of human civilization. Most of these cycles are attributed to very small variations in the Earth's orbit that change the amount of solar energy our planet receives.

The current warming trend is of particular significance because most of it is very likely human-induced and proceeding at a rate that is unprecedented in the past 1,300 years.

Earth-orbiting satellites and other technological advances have enabled scientists to see the big picture, collecting many different types of information about our planet and its climate on a global scale. This body of data, collected over many years, reveals the signals of a changing climate.

The evidence for rapid climate change is compelling:

Rise in Sea Level

Global sea level rose about 17 centimeters (6.7 inches) in the last century. The rate in the last decade, however, is nearly double that of the last century.

Global Rise in Temperature

All three major global surface temperature reconstructions show that the Earth has warmed since 1880. Most of this warming has occurred since the 1970s, with the 20 warmest years having occurred since 1981 and with all 10 of the warmest years occurring in the past 12 years. Even though the 2000s witnessed a solar output decline resulting in an unusually deep solar minimum in 2007-2009, surface temperatures continue to increase.

Warming Oceans

The oceans have absorbed much of this increased heat, with the top 700 meters (about 2,300 feet) of ocean showing warming of 0.302 degrees Fahrenheit since 1969.

Shrinking Ice Sheets

The Greenland and Antarctic ice sheets have decreased in mass. Data from NASA's Gravity Recovery and Climate Experiment show Greenland lost 150 to 250 cubic kilometers (36 to 60 cubic miles) of ice per year between 2002 and 2006, while Antarctica lost about 152 cubic kilometers (36 cubic miles) of ice between 2002 and 2005.

Declining Arctic Sea Ice

Both the extent and thickness of Arctic sea ice has declined rapidly over the last several decades.

Glacial Retreat

Glaciers are retreating or disappearing almost everywhere around the world — including in the Alps, Himalayas, Andes, Rockies, Alaska and Africa.

Extreme Events

The number of record high temperature events in the United States has been increasing, while the number of record low temperature events has been decreasing, since 1950. The U.S. has also witnessed increasing numbers of intense rainfall events.

Ocean Acidification

Since the beginning of the Industrial Revolution, the acidity of surface ocean waters has increased by about 30 percent. This increase is the result of humans emitting more carbon dioxide into the atmosphere and hence more being absorbed into the oceans. The amount of carbon dioxide absorbed by the upper layer of the oceans is increasing by about 2 billion tons per year.

Decreased Snow Cover

Satellite observations reveal that the amount of spring snow cover in the Northern Hemisphere has decreased over the past five decades and that the snow is melting earlier.

A degree of difference

So, the Earth's average temperature has increased about 1 degree Fahrenheit during the 20th century. What's the big deal?

One degree may sound like a small amount, but it's an unusual event in our planet's recent history. Earth's climate record preserved in tree rings, ice cores, and coral reefs shows that the global average temperature is stable over long periods of time. Furthermore, small changes in temperature correspond to enormous changes in the environment.

For example, at the end of the last ice age, when the Northeast United States was covered by more than 3,000 feet of ice, average temperatures were only 5 to 9 degrees cooler than today.

The Impact on our Future

Potential future effects of global climate change include more frequent wildfires, longer periods of drought in some regions and an increase in the number, duration and intensity of tropical storms.

Global climate change has already had measurable effects on the environment. Glaciers have shrunk, ice on rivers and lakes is breaking up earlier, plant and animal ranges have shifted and trees are flowering sooner.

Effects that scientists had predicted in the past would result from global climate change are now occurring: loss of sea ice, accelerated sea level rise and longer, more intense heat waves.

Scientists have high confidence that global temperatures will continue to rise for decades to come, largely due to greenhouse gases produced by human activities. The Intergovernmental Panel on Climate Change (IPCC), which includes more than 1,300 scientists from the United States and other countries, forecasts a temperature rise of 2.5 to 10 degrees Fahrenheit over the next century.

According to the IPCC, the extent of climate change effects on individual regions will vary over time and with the ability of different societal and environmental systems to mitigate or adapt to change.

The IPCC predicts that increases in global mean temperature of less than 1.8 to 5.4 degrees Fahrenheit (1 to 3 degrees Celsius) above 1990 levels will produce beneficial impacts in some regions and harmful ones in others. Net annual costs will increase over time as global temperatures increase.

"Taken as a whole," the IPCC states, "the range of published evidence indicates that the net damage costs of climate change are likely to be significant and to increase over time."

Some of the long-term effects of global climate change in the United States are as follows, according to the Third National Climate Assessment Report:

Change will continue through this century and beyond

Global climate is projected to continue to change over this century and beyond. The magnitude of climate change beyond the next few decades depends primarily on the amount of heat-trapping gases emitted globally, and how sensitive the Earth's climate is to those emissions.

Temperatures will continue to rise

Because human-induced warming is superimposed on a naturally varying climate, the temperature rise has not been, and will not be, uniform or smooth across the country or over time.

Frost-free season (and growing season) will lengthen

The length of the frost-free season (and the corresponding growing season) has been increasing nationally since the 1980s, with the largest increases occurring in the western United States, affecting ecosystems and agriculture. Across the United States, the growing season is projected to continue to lengthen.

Changes in precipitation patterns

Average U.S. precipitation has increased since 1900, but some areas have had increases greater than the national average, and some areas have had decreases. More winter and spring precipitation is projected for the northern United States, and less for the Southwest, over this century.

Projections of future climate over the U.S. suggest that the recent trend towards increased heavy precipitation events will continue. This trend is projected to occur even in regions where total precipitation is expected to decrease, such as the Southwest.

More droughts and heat waves

Droughts in the Southwest and heat waves (periods of abnormally hot weather lasting days to weeks) everywhere are projected to become more intense, and cold waves less intense everywhere.

Summer temperatures are projected to continue rising, and a reduction of soil moisture, which exacerbates heat waves, is projected for much of the western and central U.S. in summer. By the end of this century, what have been once-in-20-year extreme heat days (one-day events) are projected to occur every two or three years over most of the nation.

Hurricanes will become stronger and more intense

The intensity, frequency and duration of North Atlantic hurricanes, as well as the frequency of the strongest (Category 4 and 5) hurricanes, have all increased since the early 1980s. The relative contributions of human and natural causes to these increases are still uncertain. Hurricane-associated storm intensity and rainfall rates are projected to increase as the climate continues to warm.

Sea level will rise 1-4 feet by 2100

Global sea level has risen by about 8 inches since reliable record keeping began in 1880. It is projected to rise another 1 to 4 feet by 2100. This is the result of added water from melting land ice and the expansion of seawater as it warms.

In the next several decades, storm surges and high tides could combine with sea level rise and land subsidence to further increase flooding in many of these regions. Sea level rise will not stop in 2100 because the oceans take a very long time to respond to warmer conditions at the Earth's surface. Ocean waters will therefore continue to warm and sea level will continue to rise for many centuries at rates equal to or higher than that of the current century.

Arctic likely to become ice-free

The Arctic Ocean is expected to become essentially ice free in summer before mid-century.

Other Countries

If this is what all going to happen within United States, then consider what will be happening in rest of the parts of this world, either more or less similar conditions will prevail. So there is no such part of the world that can remain untouched by the impacts of the global climate change.

What is Triggering this Change?

Ninety-seven percent of climate scientists agree that climate-warming trends over the past century are very likely due to human activities, and most leading scientific organizations worldwide have issued public statements endorsing this position.

The heat-trapping nature of carbon dioxide and other gases was demonstrated in the mid-19th century. Their ability to affect the transfer of infrared energy through the atmosphere is the scientific basis of many instruments flown by NASA. There is no question that increased levels of greenhouse gases cause the Earth to warm in response.

Ice cores drawn from Greenland, Antarctica, and Tropical Mountain glaciers show that the Earth's climate responds to changes in greenhouse gas levels. They also show that in the past, large changes in climate have happened very quickly, geologically-speaking: in tens of years, not in millions or even thousands.

Most climate scientists agree the main cause of the current global warming trend is human expansion of the "greenhouse effect" — warming results when the atmosphere traps heat radiating from Earth toward space.

Certain gases in the atmosphere block heat from escaping. Long-lived gases that remain semi-permanently in the atmosphere and do not respond physically or chemically to changes in temperature are described as "forcing" climate change. Gases such as water vapor, which respond physically or chemically to changes in temperature, are seen as "feedbacks".

Gases that contribute to the greenhouse effect include:

Water Vapor: The most abundant greenhouse gas, but importantly, it acts as a feedback to the climate. Water vapor increases as the Earth's atmosphere warms, but so does the possibility of clouds and precipitation, making these some of the most important feedback mechanisms to the greenhouse effect.

Carbon dioxide (CO_2): A minor but very important component of the atmosphere, carbon dioxide is released through natural processes such as respiration and volcano eruptions and through human activities such as deforestation, land use changes, and burning fossil fuels. Humans have increased atmospheric CO_2 concentration by more than a third since the Industrial Revolution began. This is the most important long-lived "forcing" of climate change.

Methane: A hydrocarbon gas produced both through natural sources and human activities, including the decomposition of wastes in landfills, agriculture, and especially rice cultivation, as well as ruminant digestion and manure management associated with domestic livestock. On a molecule-for-molecule basis, methane is a far more active greenhouse gas than carbon dioxide, but also one which is much less abundant in the atmosphere.

Nitrous Oxide: A powerful greenhouse gas produced by soil cultivation practices, especially the use of commercial and organic fertilizers, fossil fuel combustion, nitric acid production, and biomass burning.

Chlorofluorocarbons (CFCs): Synthetic compounds entirely of industrial origin used in a number of applications, but now largely regulated in production and release to the atmosphere by international agreement for their ability to contribute to destruction of the ozone layer. They are also greenhouse gases.

On Earth, human activities are changing the natural greenhouse. Over the last century the burning of fossil fuels like coal and oil has increased the concentration of atmospheric carbon dioxide (CO_2). This happens because the coal or oil burning process combines carbon with oxygen in the air to make CO_2. To a lesser extent, the clearing of land for agriculture, industry, and other human activities has increased concentrations of greenhouse gases.

The consequences of changing the natural atmospheric greenhouse are difficult to predict, but certain effects seem likely:

- On average, Earth will become warmer. Some regions may welcome warmer temperatures, but others may not.

- Warmer conditions will probably lead to more evaporation and precipitation overall, but individual regions will vary, some becoming wetter and others dryer.

- A stronger greenhouse effect will warm the oceans and partially melt glaciers and other ice, increasing sea level. Ocean water also will expand if it warms, contributing further to sea level rise.

- Meanwhile, some crops and other plants may respond favorably to increased atmospheric CO2, growing more vigorously and using water more efficiently. At the same time, higher temperatures and shifting climate patterns may change the areas where crops grow best and affect the makeup of natural plant communities.

The Role of Human Activity

In its Fifth Assessment Report, the Intergovernmental Panel on Climate Change, a group of 1,300 independent scientific experts from countries all over the world under the auspices of the United Nations, concluded there's a more than 95 percent probability that human activities over the past 50 years have warmed our planet.

The industrial activities that our modern civilization depends upon have raised atmospheric carbon dioxide levels from 280 parts per million to 400 parts per million in the last 150 years. The panel also concluded there's a better than 95 percent probability that human-produced greenhouse gases such as carbon dioxide, methane and nitrous oxide have caused much of the observed increase in Earth's temperatures over the past 50 years.

Solar Irradiance

It's reasonable to assume that changes in the sun's energy output will cause climate to change, since the sun is the fundamental source of energy that drives our climate system.

Indeed, studies show that solar variability has played a role in past climate changes. For example, a decrease in solar activity is thought to have triggered the Little Ice Age between approximately 1650 and 1850, when Greenland was largely cut off by ice from 1410 to the 1720s and glaciers advanced in the Alps.

But several lines of evidence show that current global warming cannot be explained by changes in energy from the sun:

Since 1750, the average amount of energy coming from the sun either remained constant or increased slightly.

If the warming were caused by a more active sun, then scientists would expect to see warmer temperatures in all layers of the atmosphere. Instead, they have observed a cooling in the upper atmosphere, and a warming at the surface and in the lower parts of the atmosphere. That's because greenhouse gases are trapping heat in the lower atmosphere.

Climate models that include solar irradiance changes can't reproduce the observed temperature trend over the past century or more without including a rise in greenhouse gases.

How do we know that changes in the sun aren't to blame for current global warming trends?

Since 1978, a series of satellite instruments have measured the energy output of the sun directly. The satellite data show a very slight drop in solar irradiance (which is a measure of the amount of energy the sun gives off) over this time period. So the sun doesn't appear to be responsible for the warming trend observed over the past several decades.

Longer-term estimates of solar irradiance have been made using sunspot records and other so-called "proxy indicators," such as the amount of carbon in tree rings. The most recent analyses of these proxies indicate that solar irradiance changes cannot plausibly account for more than 10 percent of the 20th century's warming.

Recommendations

Below are some of the documentaries, inspiring songs, and websites that I would recommend you to watch, listen to, and visit respectively. Be sure to check them out if you haven't, they are worth watching. There are in fact many more informative sources to check out but I can't list them all here to keep it comfortable on your side. However, you can always Google "Films on Global Warming" and it will present you a whole list of films and documentaries that are intended to spread awareness, bring people together, and save Planet Earth.

This list is also available on the book's website – "www.rescueyourmom.org/recommended"

Documentaries:

The Blue Planet (2001)

The Blue Planet is a British nature documentary series created and produced by the BBC, It premiered on 12 September 2001 in the United Kingdom. It is narrated by David Attenborough. Described as "the first ever comprehensive series on the natural history of the world's oceans", each of the eight 50-minute episodes examines a different aspect of marine life. The underwater photography included creatures and behaviour that had previously never been filmed.

> *"Our planet is a blue planet: over seventy percent of it is covered by the sea. The Pacific Ocean alone covers half the globe. You can fly across it non-stop for twelve hours and still see nothing more than a speck of land. This series will reveal the complete natural history of our ocean planet, from its familiar shores to the mysteries of its deepest seas."*
>
> —*David Attenborough,* from episode one

Planet Earth (2006)

Planet Earth is a landmark 2006 British television series produced by the BBC Natural History Unit. Five years in the making, it was the most expensive nature documentary series ever commissioned by the BBC and also the first to be filmed in high definition. The series has eleven episodes, each of which features a global overview of a different biome or habitat on Earth. At the end of each fifty-minute episode, a ten-minute featurette takes a behind-the-scenes look at the challenges of filming the series.

Earth (2007)

Earth is a nature documentary film which depicts the diversity of wild habitats and creatures across the planet. The film begins in the Arctic in January of one year and moves southward, concluding in Antarctica in the December of the same year. Along the way, it features the journeys made by three particular species—the polar bear, African bush elephant and humpback whale—to highlight the threats to their survival in the face of rapid environmental change.

An Inconvenient Truth (2007)

Director Davis Guggenheim eloquently weaves the science of global warming with former Vice President Al Gore's personal history and lifelong commitment to reversing the effects of global climate change in the most talked-about documentary of the year.

An audience and critical favorite, An Inconvenient Truth makes the compelling case that global warming is real, man-made, and its effects will be cataclysmic if we don't act now. Gore presents a wide array of facts and information in a thoughtful and compelling way: often humorous, frequently emotional, and always fascinating. In the end, An Inconvenient Truth accomplishes what all great films should: it leaves the viewer shaken, involved and inspired.

Frozen Planet (2011)

Frozen Planet is a 2011 British nature documentary series, co-produced by the BBC and The Open University. It was filmed by the BBC Natural History Unit. The seven-part series focuses on life and the environment in both the Arctic and Antarctic. The production team was keen to film a comprehensive record of the natural history of the Polar Regions because climate change is affecting landforms such as glaciers, ice shelves, and the extent of sea ice.

Before the Flood (2016)

Before the Flood presents a riveting account of the dramatic changes now occurring around the world due to climate change, as well as the actions we as individuals and as a society can take to prevent catastrophic disruption of life on our planet. The film follows Leonardo DiCaprio as he travels to five continents and the Arctic speaking to scientists, world leaders, activists and local residents to gain a deeper understanding of this complex issue and investigate concrete solutions to the most pressing environmental challenge of our time.

Planet Earth II (2016)

Planet Earth II is a 2016 British nature documentary series produced by the BBC as a sequel to Planet Earth, which was broadcast in 2006. The first trailer was released on 9 October 2016, and the series premiered on 6 November 2016 in the United Kingdom. *"Experience the world from the viewpoint of animals themselves. From spellbinding wildlife spectacle to intimate encounters, Planet Earth II takes you closer than ever before."*– BBC

Earth: One Amazing Day (2017)

"Inviting you to spend 24 hours on the most amazing planet in the known universe. To witness the power of our planet, in a day that will change how you look at life. See the World in a way that will help us make connections you've never imagined. All animals are connected to the planet we call home – and shaped by the forces which drive it. Even the most familiar species – ourselves!" – BBC. It is scheduled to release on 2017 but the date still hasn't been confirmed at the time I am putting this information here.

Songs: -

Michael Jackson believed that all people are unique and equal, regardless of race or culture. His message was one of unity, harmony, and hope for a better world. Michael was a multifaceted artist who strove to fuse together various musical styles and art forms. Below are given some of his best inspiring songs that every individual must watch from kids to adults to form into a better world.

Earth Song (1995)

Michael Jackson's "Earth Song" was originally released on "HIStory: Past, Present and Future: Book I" in 1995. "Earth Song" joins such anthems as "Man in the Mirror" and "We Are the World" in demonstrating Jackson's desire for individuals to look inwardly and make the world a better place. In this instance, "Earth Song" was a plea for ecological responsibility, calling attention to the welfare of the planet's environment and wildlife.

Jackson said the inspiration for "Earth Song" came to him while he was staying in a hotel in Austria and his heart became heavy with the plight of Mother Earth. It was Jackson's belief that the Earth could feel pain from her wounds, so he wanted to write a song coming from "the voice of the planet." His "Earth Song" became the rallying cry against "man's mismanagement of the Earth." The lyrics explored themes of deforestation, pollution and war, along with wildlife concerns such as over-fishing and elephant poaching.

Though Jackson died in 2009, he left the world a powerful message of hope and change through "Earth Song." "That's why I write these kinds of songs. You know, to give some sense of awareness and awakening and hope to people. I love the planet." Jackson said. "The planet is sick. Like a fever. If we don't fix it now, it's at the point of no return. This is our last chance to fix this problem that we have. Or it's like a runaway train. And the time has come; this is it."

Man in the Mirror (1987)

In contrast to Michael's other short films of the Bad era, "Man in the Mirror" tells a story not through performance, but through powerful images of oppression, homelessness, hunger, police brutality and other ills of the world, as well as events and leaders of the 20th century whose work is reflective of the song's message to "make that change." John F. Kennedy, Martin Luther King, Jr., Mahatma Gandhi, Mother Teresa, Archbishop Desmond Tutu, Willie Nelson and Bob Geldof are among those whose humanitarian work is showcased. Michael himself is only featured briefly in a crowd shot toward the end of the film.

Heal the World (1991)

Heal The World is one of Michael Jackson's songs in the album Dangerous and HIStory: Past, Present and Future, Book I. "Heal the world" is a song about love, care and need. Michael Jackson sings to appeal to people to give their love and care to the children who are suffering from wars and poverty, making the world a better and warmer place to live. It's a moving song and lights the hope of the future for needy children. The matter of the song is to talk about life issues and world issues. The song is telling people what is going on with the world and how it can be fixed. It is written in relatively easy words so that as many people as possible can understand it.

We are the World (1985)

The charity single "We Are the World" was released on this day in 1985, and became a global #1 hit, selling more than 20 million copies and raising funds for famine and medical relief in Africa. The song, written by Michael Jackson and Lionel Richie, was recorded by an all-star supergroup at A&M Recording Studios in Hollywood where they all gathered following the live telecast of the American Music Awards. The "We Are The World" single and album, combined with other promotional activities, raised more than $60 million for humanitarian aid (equivalent to more than $130 million today) through the non-profit USA For Africa which continues its work today.

Websites: -

Before the Flood – www.beforetheflood.com

NASA Climate – www.climate.nasa.gov

NASA Earth – www.nasa.gov/earth

NASA Ice – www.ice.nasa.gov

Save the Arctic – www.savethearctic.org

Follow these organizations on twitter to be alert of climate change and possible solutions: -

Rainforest Action Network (@RAN), NASA Climate (@NASAClimate), NASA Earth (@NASAEarth), NASA Ice (@NASA_ICE), Save the Arctic (@SavetheArctic), Arctic Sunrise (@gp_sunrise), World Wildlife Fund (@World_Worldlife), and so on for the rest that you find helpful.

Please visit the websites of the organizations I have mentioned previously, and lend them your support. Their websites have a separate page featuring what action you can take: most of them require just your vote, signature, name, email, or a message to send and share it on social media. In some cases, there is only one way to help them and that is by donating any amount you wish. They are always in need of our generous support for making our home beautiful and safe. Whatever the help, lend a hand and ***keep yourself always active and engaged*** in the activities of these organizations as well as your own, so that you miss no chance to save this planet.

We can share news of these activities and information on animal welfare and climate change on social media. Think about it. ***You can make the change happen.*** Every child can do something for his/her mother. You are the responsible citizen as well as a child of Mother Earth.

Afterword

I highly recommend that you purchase this book, even if it is a pirated copy. By doing so, you will help contribute to this planet's protection and welfare. If you can afford it, please purchase several copies of the book, and distribute it to those who cannot afford it. When you purchase a digital edition of this book, such as an eBook, it's even better – your money goes more towards the environment than incurring the expenses of printing and paper costs, which consume a lot of funds and natural resources. Obviously, printing uses paper, as well as energy, which we certainly prefer to avoid. Do whatever is reasonable, helpful, and useful. Overall, remember, all we need to do is—save this planet—our mom.

The Cover Story

This is the story of a girl who discovers that a forest is about to be cleared, which is home to so many animals and birds living there that she cannot stop herself and runs out from her home, barefoot, to save the forest. The man in charge of this operation was none other than her dad who walks through the forest to find a place to begin his work. But as soon as he reaches the forest with his friend and raises his axe to cut down a tree, he finds his daughter sitting at the foot of the tree covering Mother Earth with her body, ensuring protection to the forest and all its creatures. He is taken aback. She looks at him and says, "Daddy, I love you a lot, but you can end my life first if you want to go ahead with clearing this forest and making the animals homeless. Yes daddy, this forest is my life, and all these innocent animals are my friends. In fact, the forest is home to so many wonderful creatures. Don't you see it, Daddy?" Looking into her twinkling eyes filled with endless hope, he becomes speechless, falling down on knees like he has lost all his energy to argue with his daughter. She is loving Mother Earth in such a way as if she herself is a mother and the earth her daughter. She seems to be a part of the forest. The animals approach her to take a look and cherish the moment together, for she is protecting their beautiful home—the home in which they live.

Her dad starts to realize his mistake and feels quite guilty for everything he has done to the environment till now. He had no idea how many lives had been destroyed, how many lost their home, and all because of his desire to earn a livelihood at the cost of lives of other species on this planet. Now he understands, if he does not stop harming the environment anymore, it is sure, his own daughter would be killed. He understands that destroying the earth and its environment for money and luxuries would simply mean destruction of the lives of his own children, and hence his own. He realizes that he must stop and drop his weapons, and be thankful to his daughter for making him realize what is more important in life. By protecting this planet, she wasn't protecting just one, but all lives that flourish on earth, including her own.

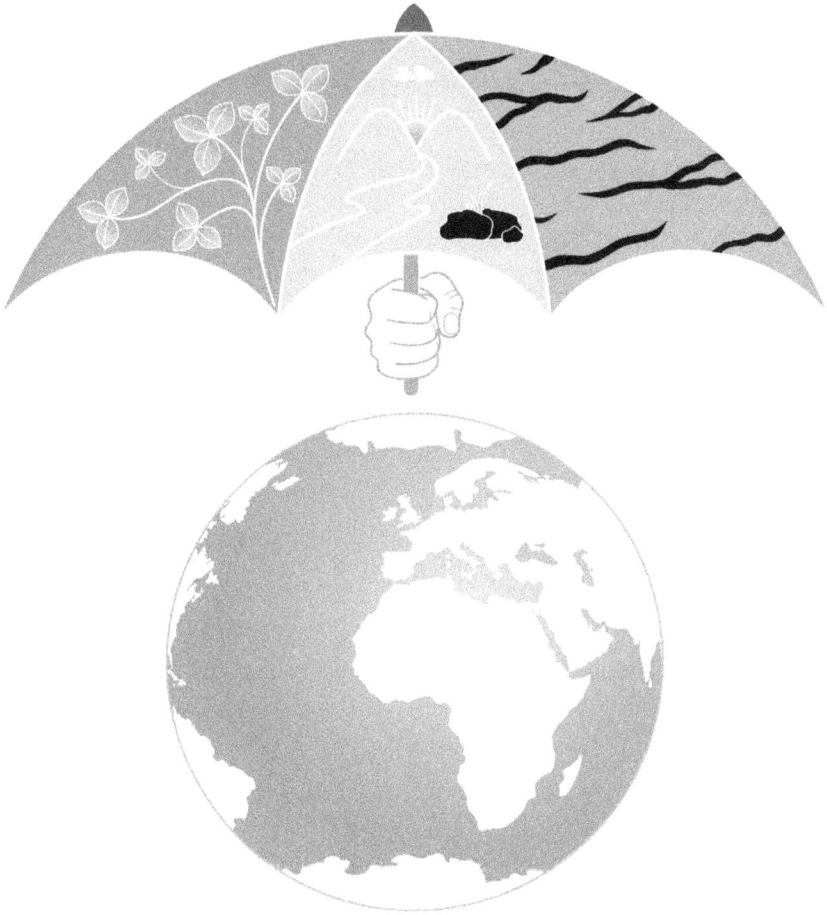

Above is the symbol of "*Rescue Your Mom*", representing *Mother Earth* with a protecting *Umbrella* which is made up of three components—the *Greenery*, the *Biosphere*, and the *Wildlife*, and the responsibility to keep this umbrella intact is in our hands—so is the hand holding it. Our earth is safe until this precious umbrella is safe. If there occurs any damage to this umbrella (to any of its three components), our earth will be soon exposed to danger and this will threaten the existence of all the living species on this planet including human beings. Hence, we need to keep this precious umbrella safe. Help protect it now!

Bibliography

Reference Websites: -

- NASA Climate (www.climate.nasa.gov)
- Rainforest Action Network (www.ran.org)
- The New Mexico Solar Energy Association (www.nmsea.org)
- Better Palm Oil (www.betterpalmoil.org)
- Wikipedia (www.en.wikipedia.org)
- BBC (www.bbc.co.uk)
- Disney Nature (www.nature.disney.com)
- Michael Jackson Official Website (www.michaeljackson.com)
- Michael Jackson.com (www.allmichaeljackson.com)
- Entertainment Guide (www.entertainmentguide.local.com)
- Gymnasium Steglitz Berlin (www.gs.cidsnet.de/englisch-online/ Grundkurs4/modernlyrics.htm)
- Academia (www.academia.edu)
- Al Gore (www.algore.com)
- BrainyQuote (www.brainyquote.com)
- Websites of all the organizations mentioned in this book.

Reference Videos: -

- Planet Earth (2006)
- Before the Flood (2016)

I became an author to help save our Mother Earth.
What are you going to contribute?

Now it is up to you to become part of the change.

www.ingramcontent.com/pod-product-compliance
Lightning Source LLC
Chambersburg PA
CBHW030839090426
42737CB00009B/1033